# PICTORIAL
## SUPPLEMENT TO
## LMS LOCOMOTIVE PROFILE No. 5
### THE MIXED TRAFFIC CLASS 5s
### – Nos. 5000–5224

by JOHN JENNISON & DAVID CLARKE
with DAVID HUNT, FRED JAMES
& BOB ESSERY

WILD SWAN PUBLICATIONS

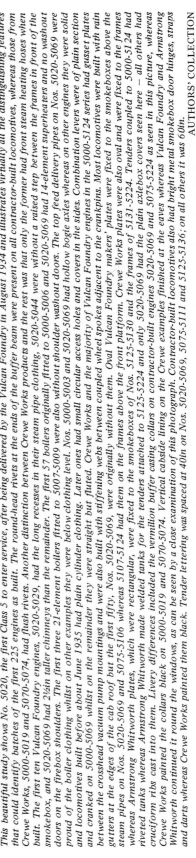

This beautiful study shows No. 5020, the first Class 5 to enter service, after being delivered by the Vulcan Foundry in August 1934 and illustrates virtually all the distinguishing features that could identify batches of the first 225 engines as built. The round-head rivets at the ends of the buffer beam were present on all contractor-built locomotives, whereas those from Crewe Works, 5000-5019 and 5070-5074, had flush rivets. Another distinction between Crewe Works products and the rest was that only the former had front steam heating hoses when built. The first ten Vulcan Foundry engines, 5020-5029, had the long recesses in their steam pipe clothing, 5020-5044 were without a raised step between the frames in front of the smokebox, and 5020-5069 had 2½in taller chimneys than the remainder. The first 57 boilers originally fitted to 5000-5006 and 5020-5069 had 14-element superheaters and no washout doors on the firebox shoulders. The first three 21-element boilers fitted to 5007-5009 were also without shoulder washout doors. The top feed delivery pipes on Nos. 5020-5069 were solid proud of the boiler clothing whilst on other examples they were below clothing level. Nos. 5000-5003 and 5020-5069 had hollow bogie axles whereas on other engines they were solid and locomotives built before about June 1935 had plain cylinder clothing. Later ones had small circular access holes and covers in the sides. Combination levers were of plain section and cranked on 5000-5069 whilst on the remainder they were straight but fluted. Crewe Works and the majority of Vulcan Foundry engines in the 5000-5124 series had gusset plates between the crosshead vacuum pump mountings and were also built with stiffening webs between coupled wheel spokes adjacent to the crankpins. Most locomotives were built with rain gutters at the edges of the cab roof but the first fifty, Nos. 5020-5069, were originally without them. Oval Vulcan Foundry makers' plates were fixed to the smokeboxes above the steam pipes on Nos. 5020-5069 and 5075-5106 whereas 5107-5124 had them on the frames above the front platform. Crewe Works plates were also oval and were fixed to the frames whereas Armstrong Whitworth plates, which were rectangular, were fixed to the smokeboxes of Nos. 5125-5130 and the frames of 5131-5224. Tenders coupled to 5000-5124 had riveted tanks whereas Armstrong Whitworth made welded tanks for the tenders attached to 5125-5224 and only 5020-5069 had the plain axlebox covers seen here – all others had cruciform ribs cast into them. Livery differences included the vermilion buffer casing collars on contractor-built engines 5020-5069 and 5075-5224 as seen in this picture, whereas Crewe Works painted the collars black on 5000-5019 and 5070-5074. Vertical cabside lining on the Crewe examples finished at the eaves whereas Vulcan Foundry and Armstrong Whitworth continued it round the windows, as can be seen by a close examination of this photograph. Contractor-built locomotives also had bright metal smokebox door hinges, straps and darts whereas Crewe Works painted them black. Tender lettering was spaced at 40in on Nos. 5020-5069, 5075-5111 and 5125-5136; on all others it was 60in.

# INTRODUCTION

*During the mid-1930s, Class 5s were used in various trials. Some involved taking cylinder indicator diagrams, and shelters were built onto the front of a locomotive for the protection of engineers who operated pressure recording equipment, a typical example being that seen on 5051. The engine shows all the characteristics of the Vulcan Foundry 5020-5069 series as described elsewhere, including tall chimney and external top feed delivery pipes, and was coupled to a Mk 1 riveted tender with plain axlebox covers. It was in charge of a 'Maltese' train that was officially classified by the LMS as No. 5 and described as 'Express freight or cattle train with the continuous brake on less than one-third of the vehicles but in use on four vehicles connected to the engine'.* A. G. ELLIS

This book is intended primarily to be referred to alongside *LMS Locomotive Profile No. 5*, which contains a detailed discussion of the origins and development of the first 225 Class 5s. Since some readers may not have that volume, a very brief overview will be given here.

By the time W. A. Stanier took charge of locomotive affairs on the LMS in 1932, there was an urgent and pressing requirement for more examples of reliable, economical mixed traffic engines. The Horwich moguls were proving their worth and the Traffic Department wanted more of them but Stanier and the Locomotive Department had other ideas. The immediate need was addressed by production of forty more moguls to what was basically the 1925 design revised to include some of Stanier's ideas, including a new, higher-pressure taper boiler that enabled a reduction in cylinder diameter and their repositioning without fouling the loading gauge. The long-term solution to the company's requirement, however, lay in development of a Class 5 engine of increased power and the adoption of a scrap and build policy to replace many of the more elderly and less economical types inherited from the pre-Grouping constituent companies.

Various proposals were schemed before the design of a 4–6–0 that could run over at least 70% of the LMS system was finalised. Volume production was needed to meet the new acquisition policy and tenders were invited from outside contractors. The first order to be placed was with the Vulcan Foundry of Newton-le-Willows, followed by a larger order to Armstrong Whitworth as well as production at Crewe Works. Although Government loans at favourable rates of interest were provided for the construction of later Class 5s,

LMS committee minutes that we have examined do not make it clear whether this applied to any of the first 225 engines that were built as follows:

| Numbers | Makers | Delivered |
|---|---|---|
| 5000–5019 | Crewe Works | Feb 35–May 35 |
| 5020–5069 | Vulcan Foundry | Aug 34–Jan 35 |
| 5070–5074 | Crewe Works | May 35–Jun 35 |
| 5075–5124 | Vulcan Foundry | Feb 35–Jul 35 |
| 5125–5224 | Armstrong Whitworth | Apr 35–Dec 35 |

New locomotives usually went to Crewe for breaking in before being allocated to one of the four LMS operating divisions. The first ten locomotives went to the Northern Division (Scotland), but thereafter they were allocated to all the divisions, with the Western Division receiving the largest number. Early transfers changed the divisional balance but in due course examples of the entire class could be found over most of the LMS system. Tables of allocations can be found in *LMS Locomotive Profile No. 5*.

As with discussion of origins and development, *LMS Locomotive Profile No. 5* contains detailed descriptions of the engines' construction, components and modifications, so only a very brief overview will be included here. We will concentrate on those aspects of construction and alterations that had an obvious effect on the external appearance of the engines. Some other, less noticeable, external details are pointed out in the photograph captions and we would refer readers to the *Profile* for internal ones. Explanations of the construction and working of the various components and fittings, as well as reasons for alterations, are also in the *Profile*.

A common practice with many railway companies and contractors was to take a series of official photographs showing one member of a class successively renumbered to represent some or all of the remainder. This study of what appears at first glance to be No. 5000 illustrates the point. The locomotive shown had circular access plates in its cylinder clothing, solid bogie axles, straight combination lever and a 21-element boiler with washout doors on its firebox shoulders, none of which applied to 5000. Furthermore, the tender shown was a standard riveted Mk 1 whereas 5000 was coupled to a rebuilt tender from one of the first three 4–6–2s, which had a different side profile and rivet pattern as well as roller bearing axleboxes. From these clues, plus the presence of a vacuum pump gasset plate, we would estimate that the engine was actually one of the second Vulcan Foundry batch in the 5100–5110 series that had been renumbered and fitted with a Crewe Works plate. The photograph illustrates nicely the relationship between firebox tubeplate and driving axle on locomotives carrying vertical-throatplate boilers. On those with sloping-throatplate boilers, the tubeplate was further forward in line with the axle.          NRM (DY20043)

*The second batch of Vulcan Foundry engines, Nos. 5075-5124 built between February and July 1935, differed from their predecessors in several respects. This photograph of No. 5097 in works grey illustrates some of them. Most important, though probably least obvious, was the fact that the boiler contained twenty-one superheater elements rather than fourteen, the only indication of which was the presence of shoulder washout doors on the firebox. The chimney was shorter than before, bogie axles were solid, the combination lever was straight and fluted, there were no stiffening webs on coupled wheel spokes, edges of the cab roof were bent up to form rain gutters, and water pipes to the top feed were below boiler clothing level with flat covering strips. The first thirty of the new batch, including 5097, still had their makers' plates on the smokebox. The only difference between tenders was that the second batch had cruciform ribs cast onto the faces of their axlebox covers, as shown here. Livery was the same as before, including 40in letter spacing on the tender sides.*

AUTHORS' COLLECTION

*The largest order for vertical-throatplate Class 5s was placed with Armstrong Whitworth and the engines were delivered between April and December 1935. The first of them, No. 5125, is seen here in photographic grey livery. The locomotives were the same as the second batch of Vulcan Foundry examples, having 21-element boilers with firebox shoulder washout doors, short chimneys, top feed delivery pipes below clothing level, solid bogie axles, and rain gutters on the cab roofs. Like the second batch of Vulcan Foundry engines, Nos. 5125-5224 had no gusset plates between the crosshead vacuum pump mountings and their combination levers were straight and fluted. Early examples had plain cylinder clothing and the first six had makers' plates on the smokeboxes as seen here. Characteristics they share with all the other 125 engines as built included clips at the fronts of the cylinder drain pipes, hollow coupled axles, gravity sanding, and hot-water de-sanding. Their tender tanks were welded rather than riveted construction, as shown by the lack of rivet heads on the side, pipes, hollow coupled axles, gravity sanding, and hot-water de-sanding. Their tender tanks were welded rather than riveted construction, as shown by the lack of rivet heads on the side, and axlebox covers had cruciform ribs on them. The lining and transfers on the engine in this picture give the impression that it was about to be painted in LMS lake but this is erroneous – all Class 5s were black.*

AUTHORS' COLLECTION

The first Class 5s to be delivered were Nos. 5020-5069 built at the Vulcan Foundry of Newton-le-Willows between August 1934 and January 1935. They differed in some respects from the other engines and some of the differences can be seen in this splendid photograph of No. 5041 in original condition. The chimney was 2½in taller than the type fitted to other locomotives in the class, the water delivery pipes to the top feed clacks were outside the boiler clothing and covered from halfway up the boiler by fairings, and there were no rain gutters at the edges of the cab roof. The first twenty-five of them, including 5041, were built without a step between the frames in front of the smokebox and all fifty had hollow bogie axles, which were also used on the initial four Crewe Works examples. Other features that they shared with the first twenty Crewe Works products were the gusset plate between the cross-head vacuum pump mountings, plain section, cranked combination levers and stiffening webs at the rear of the coupled wheel spokes adjacent to the crankpins. The first eighty Vulcan Foundry and initial six Armstrong Whitworth locomotives had their makers' plates fixed to the smokebox just above the steam pipes. Characteristics of all the outside contractor-built engines were the two round-head rivets at either end of the buffer beam and lack of front steam-heating equipment. The boiler was one of the first fifty-seven made with 14-element superheaters and is seen here before being modified with 24 elements and a dome. Note the lack of washout doors on the shoulder of the firebox and large cover over both the atomiser steam cock and the lubricator union for the regulator on the rear of the smokebox. As with all 225 locomotives as built, the smokebox had relatively few rivet heads on the wrapper and none on the door ring, the reasons for which are explained elsewhere, and there was no door support bracket on the right-hand* side. Also common to all the engines as built were plain cylinder clothing, clips and brackets at the fronts of the cylinder drain pipes, hollow coupled axles, flush-riveted balance weights, gravity sanding, and hot-water de-sanding apparatus. The tender was a Mk 1 riveted version, which was also the type coupled to all other Crewe Works and Vulcan Foundry engines when built. The first fifty of the latter firm's tenders, however, had the plain axlebox covers seen here. The only livery difference between Crewe and contractors' tenders was the spacing of the letters, which on Vulcan Foundry and Armstrong Whitworth's products was initially 40in as seen here. There was also a difference in the cab side lining but this feature is not visible in this photograph.

T. G HEPBURN

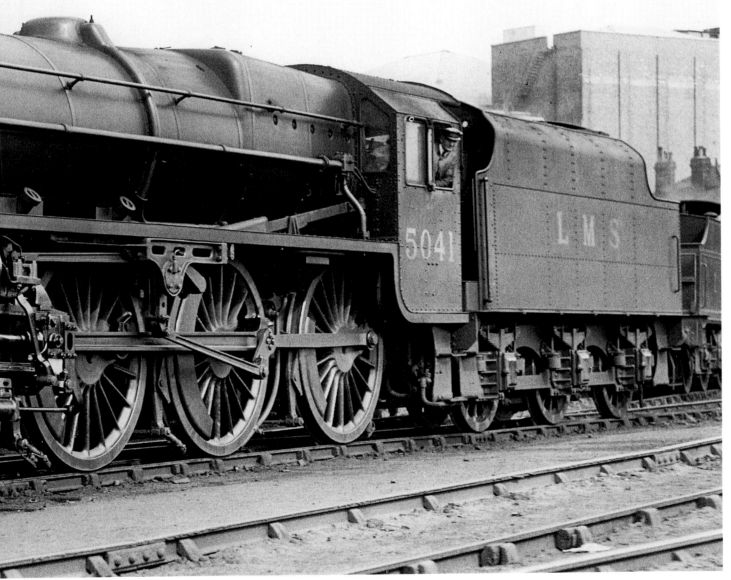

*Right- or left-hand is determined by standing on the footplate and looking forward.

This photograph was taken at Perth in 1936 and shows one of the engines built at Crewe Works in the early part of 1935 still in its original condition. On the platform between firebox and smokebox were several labelled components and an oil can, the former presumably awaiting refitting, and the tube cleaner cock had been removed from the side of the smokebox. Characteristic of Crewe locomotives were the flush-riveted buffer beam and front steam heating hose, although the latter were sometimes fitted retrospectively to contractor-built engines. The chimney was one of the shorter variety fitted to all except the first fifty Vulcan Foundry engines and the small recess just visible in the steam pipe clothing above the platform was common to all except the first ten from that firm. No. 5003 was one of four Crewe-built locomotives to have hollow bogie axles and, as with all but the first twenty-five Vulcan Foundry engines, was made with a step between the frames in front of the smokebox. The tender differed from the first fifty Vulcan Foundry Mk Is in having cruciform ribs cast into its axlebox covers and had 60in letter spacing.

AUTHORS' COLLECTION

One of only four Class 5s to be named in LMS or BR service was Armstrong Whitworth No. 5158. Built in July 1935, it was named Glasgow Yeomanry in May 1936 while stationed at St. Rollox. Some characteristics of Armstrong Whitworth and the second batch of Vulcan Foundry engines can be clearly seen in this photograph including washout doors on the firebox shoulders of the 21-element boiler, straight, fluted combination lever, vacuum pump mountings without gusset plate, solid bogie axles, and cab roof rain gutters. Differences included the fact that from 5131 onwards, the makers' plates were mounted on the frames and on locomotives built after about June 1935, access holes with small circular covers were provided in the cylinder clothing for the steam chest drain and oil pipe adapter for the top barrel feed, both of which are evident here. As with all contractor-built engines, the two rivets at each end of the buffer beam were round-headed. The tender was a welded Mk 2. The photograph also provides a good reference for the black, lined vermilion livery except that 5158 had been repainted by the time it was taken. When new, the cab windows of contractor-built engines were lined, whereas in this picture they weren't. Note the bright metal cylinder and valve chest covers, wheel bosses, outside faces of tyres and reverser reach rod. When built, the smokebox door hinges, straps and dart would also have been bright metal but became black when the engine was repainted. The vermilion buffer casing collars indicate that repainting was not carried out at Crewe where, following LNWR practice, they would have been painted black. The background colour to Armstrong Whitworth makers' plates was, we believe, red at this time.

AUTHORS' COLLECTION

The characteristics of an Armstrong Whitworth engine are evident in this study of 5167 following delivery in August 1935. Points to note include the straight and fluted combination lever, lack of gusset plate on the vacuum pump, firebox shoulder washout doors, and welded tender. Not being one of the first Armstrong Whitworth engines, the rectangular makers' plates were on the front frames and tender lettering was spaced at 60in. This engine is seen in its original livery.

AUTHORS' COLLECTION

No. 5094, built by Vulcan Foundry in 1935, is seen here at Crewe following delivery from the builders. As we would expect, the Vulcan works plate is visible on the side of the smokebox, the smokebox door hinges were polished and a vacuum pump was fitted. The boiler was domeless with feed pipes concealed by the boiler clothing and two washout plugs can be seen on the firebox shoulders. The riveted tender had ribbed covers on the axleboxes and there were no plates on the cylinder clothing. The holes in the driving wheel axles can be seen, but the bogie axles were solid. Compare with an earlier engine from the same builder, No. 5041, which is shown on pages 6/7.

PHOTOMATIC

# LOCOMOTIVES IN DETAIL

Although there were numerous variations between members of the class, from an operating standpoint a Class 5 was a Class 5. Permitted loadings over given sections of line were clearly set out in the company's *Loading of Passenger and Freight Trains* books, which did not differentiate between batches of locomotives, and we have not found any official recognition of differences in steam-generating properties between the various boilers fitted to the class. All were allocated to power class 5 and we think it safe to assume that all were considered to be of equal power and performance when being rostered to work trains. At individual sheds, the most important work would be allocated to locomotives in the best condition, regardless of whether they had a vertical or sloping throatplate boiler or any other variations. Working railwaymen would be aware of the potential of each locomotive and, although there was really no such thing as a bad Class 5, some would be recognised as being better than others. These differences were largely due to mileage run since intermediate or general overhaul and standards of maintenance at the home shed.

As we will see, there were variations between the lots as built as well as between individual locomotives within those lots but to the enginemen very few made any practical difference. It didn't really matter if one engine had a chimney that was 2½ inches taller than another, if axles were solid or hollow, tender tanks were riveted or welded, or how engine and tender were painted. What would interest the engine crews were such things as the absence of a front step enabling men of shorter stature easily to reach the lamp holder on the smokebox door or the presence of rain gutters that prevented water from dropping down their necks when they were looking out of the cab windows, which they spent a lot of time doing. Although the arrangement for washout doors would not affect the enginemen, it would be of considerable concern to the boiler washers, who would have little interest in whether the locomotive was fitted for gravity or steam sanding. The latter, however, would be of great interest to a fireman as engines with gravity sanding used rather more sand than those equipped with steam sanding, which could

make the difference between having to make one or two trips from the sand oven carrying heavy containers when preparing one for duty.

We could continue but the point has been made. There were, however, many detail variations that were incorporated for sound mechanical, operational or maintenance reasons. In this section we illustrate many of those we have identified that applied to the subjects of this volume.

The first 225 engines were built with vertical-throatplate Type 3B boilers of various internal arrangements, all being domeless initially. Those fitted to Nos. 5000–5006 and 5020–5069 had 14-element superheaters but were found to be less economical than was desired and so a 21-element version was produced. This type was fitted to 5007–5019 and 5070–5224 from new and eventually the 14-element versions were rebuilt to have 24 elements and domes, the 21-element examples remaining domeless throughout their lives.

Boilers were fed by a live steam injector inside the left-hand cab footstep support

*No. 5005 was built at Crewe in August 1935, whereupon it was photographed as seen here. The use of countersunk rivets on the ends of the buffer beam and front steam heating equipment at this time identify it as a Crewe Works product. The principal reason for fitting steam heating at the front was probably for hauling carriages tender-first both whilst in revenue-earning service and with empty stock that would make up a service train. Letters of complaint about the lack of heating in trains were not popular with the Traffic Department management, so it was normal practice to heat the carriages before passenger joined the train at its starting point. This photograph shows the stabilising strap that reinforced the front step, and the steam lance cock in a lower position compared with the view of 45084 on page 18.* AUTHORS' COLLECTION

These two photographs, together with the one on page 68 of LMS Locomotive Profiles No. 5 illustrate some of the boiler changes that took place and show Crewe Works No. 5011 at three times in its life between being built in April 1935 and withdrawn in December 1965. Apart from two periods, the first being December 1942-November 1943 and the second January 1949-October 1954, it carried vertical-throatplate, domeless boilers.

In LMS Locomotive Profiles No. 5, No. 5011 is seen taking water at Tain carrying its original vertical-throatplate, 21-element boiler with firebox shoulder washout doors. Unaltered since being built, except for the addition of an automatic tablet exchanger on the cab side, the engine was typical of Crewe Works products with an all flush-riveted buffer beam, front steam heating equipment, and makers' plates on the frames above the front platform.

The top photograph on this page shows the same engine at Perth during April 1949, three months after being renumbered 45011, with the sloping-throatplate, 28-element, domed boiler, having the top feed on the first ring that it carried from January 1949 to October 1954. As far as we know, No. 45011 was one of only five engines in the 5000-5224 series to have been fitted with such boilers. Note the extra washout plug just behind the smokebox above the handrail with which all such boilers were made. Apart from the boiler, the engine exhibited several alterations since it was built. Among them was what appears to have been a new smokebox with extra liner plates at the front, as shown by the rivet heads on the door ring, a hinged crossbar into which the dart engaged, shown by the short parallel rows of rivets halfway up the front of the wrapper, and a support bracket for the door on the right-hand side. The smokebox was also self-cleaning, which was indicated by the SC plate immediately below the shed code. This meant that there was no need for the fireman to open the smokebox door each time the locomotive came onto the shed for fire and ashpan cleaning. The ashes were ejected into the air and any residue in the smokebox was removed when the locomotive came due for boiler washout. The atomiser steam cock had been moved down to below the handrail and, since the boiler had a dome-mounted regulator, there was no need for a lubricator union so the cover was smaller than that originally fitted. Round-head rivets had replaced the flush ones originally used to secure the ends of the buffer beam to the platform angles, the crosshead vacuum pump had been removed, and the cylinder clothing had a large circular access cover on the side and two rectangular ones on the shoulder. The latter were for access to the valve chest atomised oil unions and liner securing bolts. Steam sanding had been

fitted, hot-water de-sanding gear removed, and the driving axle replaced with a solid example (the apparently small hole in the axle was actually a centre for machining the wheels). The balance weight on the driving wheel had been repaired using round-head countersunk rivets and an automatic tablet exchanger was fitted to the cab side. In 1943, a spare set of frames was made at Crewe and from then on, frame exchanges were frequent. In this picture, Crewe-built 45011 is carrying Armstrong Whitworth makers' plates on its frames above the front platform, indicating that they were originally fitted to one of that firm's engines built after June 1935. Livery was early BR lined black with Gill Sans smokebox door numbers, cabside numbers and 'BRITISH RAILWAYS' on the tender sides, the cabside numerals being set high enough to clear the tablet exchanger. The engine was coupled to a riveted tender.

The bottom picture shows 45011 in its final condition as running in the mid-1960s when stationed at Polmadie. It had reverted to a 21-element, vertical-throatplate boiler but the top feed cover was still the later-pattern transverse one that it had received with its previous boiler. Extra washout plugs had been fitted immediately behind the smokebox on top of the barrel. Its buffer beam once more had flush rivets at the ends and had been drilled for the attachment of a snowplough, the fixing bolts for which can be seen between the buffers. All the axles were solid and all balance weights had been repaired using round-head rivets. AWS was fitted, as shown by the receiver guard under the buffer beam and vacuum reservoir on the platform in front of the cab, and the locomotive was coupled to a Mk 2 welded tender. Livery was standard BR lined black, except for the lack of vermilion lining on the cylinder clothing bands, with post-1956 crests and overhead electrification warning flashes on the front frames, firebox shoulders and tender front.                    AUTHORS' COLLECTION

plate and an exhaust steam injector on the right between the frames. Nos. 5020–5069 had the delivery pipes to the top feed clacks outside the boiler clothing under separate covers whereas on the remainder they were under cover strips flush with the clothing panels. Subsequently, Nos. 5020–5069 were modified to conform with the rest of the class.

LMS 'pop' type safety valves and a horizontal whistle were mounted on top of the firebox and a blow-off cock was fitted on the left-hand side near the front of the firebox. All the 14-element boilers, the first three 21-element boilers made at Crewe, and the rebuilt 24-element, domed boilers just had washout plugs on the firebox sides. The majority of the 21-element boilers originally fitted to Nos. 5010–5019 and 5070 onwards, however, also had two washout inspection doors with small domed covers on each shoulder of the firebox. In later years, extra washout plugs were fitted at the front of the barrel. When an engine underwent a general repair, it normally lost its boiler and was fitted with the first available serviceable one. Thus, the type of boiler seen on any particular locomotive could change every few years. The firebox and boiler clothing panels, however, usually stayed with the locomotive rather than going with the boiler, which meant that once an engine had been fitted with a boiler having a dome or firebox shoulder washout doors, the panels would subsequently often have blanking plates if it reverted to a boiler without either of them. After 1937, some engines had their frames altered to receive the later type of 3B boiler with a sloping throatplate and dome, further locomotives were altered later, and from 1943 frames were exchanged during routine repairs so that eventually many locomotives carried sloping-throatplate boilers at one time or another. Full details of boiler changes will be found in the *Profile*.

A tube cleaner cock was positioned on the right-hand side of the smokebox near the base, and a streamlined cover near the top on the left-hand side housed an atomiser steam cock as well as the regulator lubricator pipe on domeless boilers. Later, the positions of the tube cleaner cocks and atomisers varied, as shown in the photographs, and boilers with dome-mounted regulators rendered the lubricators superfluous. In the later BR period some locomotives had the tube cleaner steam cocks mounted lower down with a union near the top of the smokebox and an external steam pipe between them. Chimneys originally fitted to 5020–5069 were 2½ in taller than those on the remainder of the class. In later years, some engines were fitted with a door support bracket on the right-hand side of the smokebox.

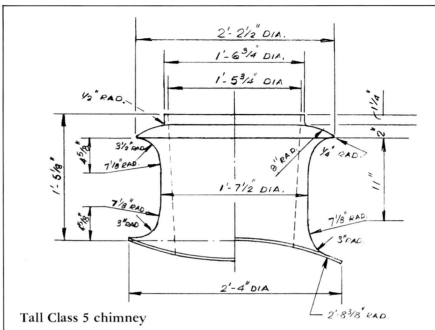

**Tall Class 5 chimney**

*The first fifty locomotives to be built, Nos. 5020-5069, were fitted when new with the slightly taller type of chimney shown here. In due course, they were equipped with the design of chimney shown below.*

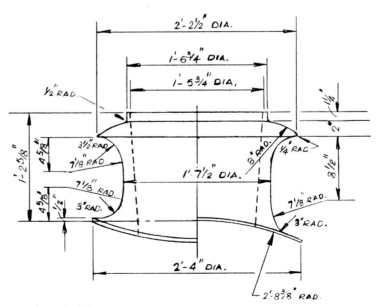

**Short Class 5 chimney**

*With the exception of the first fifty Vulcan Foundry engines, Nos. 5050-5069, this pattern of chimney was fitted to the entire class when built and was also used on the first fifty locomotives when replacements were needed.*

FRED JAMES

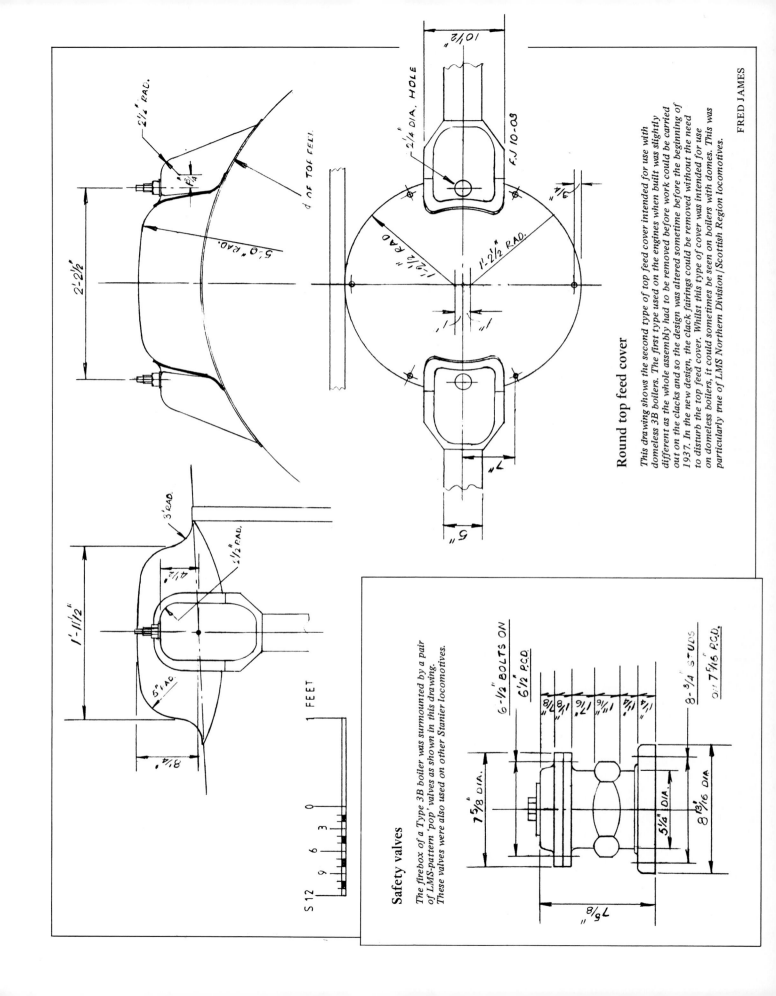

## Round top feed cover

*This drawing shows the second type of top feed cover intended for use with domeless 3B boilers. The first type used on the engines when built was slightly different as the whole assembly had to be removed before work could be carried out on the clacks and so the design was altered sometime before the beginning of 1937. In the new design, the clack fairings could be removed without the need to disturb the top feed cover. Whilst this type of cover was intended for use on domeless boilers, it could sometimes be seen on boilers with domes. This was particularly true of LMS Northern Division/Scottish Region locomotives.*

FRED JAMES

## Safety valves

*The firebox of a Type 3B boiler was surmounted by a pair of LMS-pattern 'pop' valves as shown in this drawing.
These valves were also used on other Stanier locomotives.*

Working locomotives in preservation do not always represent the condition in which they were withdrawn from British Railways service. We feel it important to make this clear so that readers, particularly model makers, do not use pictures of preserved locomotives as the basis for anything other than what they are. One of us recalls a footplate trip on an ex-LMS engine where certain controls were very unfamiliar. Many years had passed since he had been on this class of locomotive, but surely these fittings were incorrect? Curiosity prevailed and the question was asked. The answer was simple – 'We needed the fitting in order to keep the engine in service but could not get an ex-LMS example so we used one from Swindon'. Another example is that most preserved engines today are fitted with GWR-style injectors. Therefore, taking preserved locomotives as representative of how they would have looked prior to withdrawal from British Railways service is not always valid. Our policy, therefore, is not to use pictures of locomotives in preservation unless there is no other way of illustrating a particular feature. This photograph is a case in point and, whilst it shows 45110 after preservation, nothing visible had been changed materially since it ran in BR ownership although there are a couple of details that are different from the engine drawings. The picture shows a wealth of detail not often apparent. The small circular plates in the boiler clothing just in front of the top feed covered two washout plugs that were originally intended for cleaning the feedwater trays and therefore did not need the frequent access that other, uncovered plugs required. They were first fitted to new sloping-throat-plate boilers in about 1937 and not many domeless boilers were modified to have them. Details of the circular top feed cover and separately removable clack fairings can clearly be seen, as can details of the boiler clothing and bands. Note that the clothing panels behind the top feed were arranged with the right overlapping the left whereas the others were the opposite way around and that, unlike the firebox clothing, there were no screws attaching them to the crinoline bars beneath. As designed, all the panels were supposed to have been arranged with the left overlapping the right at the top and should have been screwed down. It can also be seen that the cover strips for the delivery pipes to the top feed were not absolutely flat but were slightly raised in the centre. Whilst the majority, apart from the first fifty Vulcan Foundry engines when originally built, had the pipes fully recessed under flat covers, the type seen here was not unknown. The offset between left and right firebox shoulder washout doors is readily apparent, as are the washout plugs immediately forward of the firebox on the second ring of the barrel. The cab roof ventilator, which was rarely closed, can be seen together with holes in the cab front plate that provided additional ventilation.

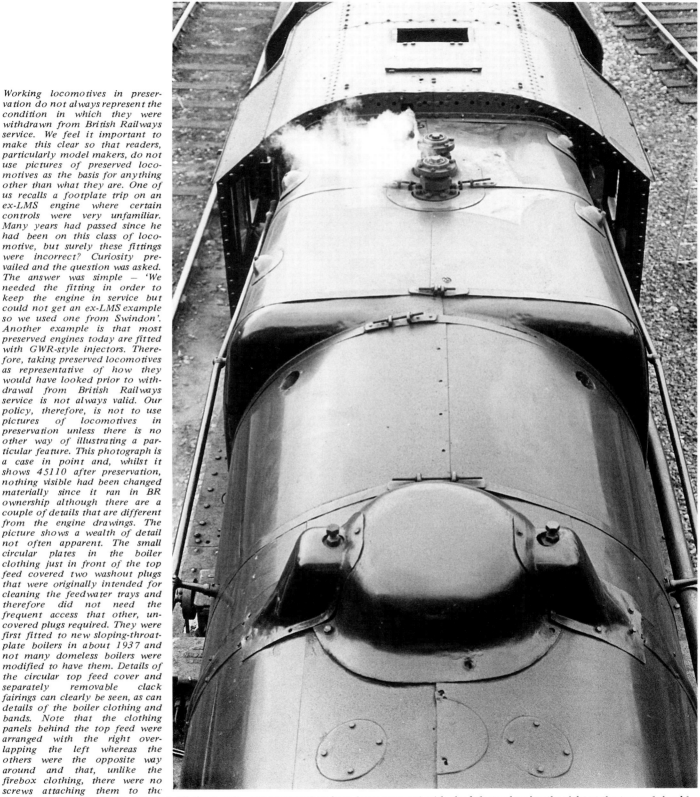

AUTHORS' COLLECTION

*Over the years, many alterations were made to Class 5s. No. 5005 was built at Crewe Works in March 1935 and was photographed sometime between nationalisation in January 1948 and having its BR number applied the following September. During the intervening years its cylinder clothing had been fitted with circular and rectangular access covers, round-head rivets had been used at the ends of the buffer beam, the tube cleaner cock had been positioned higher on the smokebox, and the smokebox itself had been fitted with long liner plates as shown by the extra rivets. Its original 14-element boiler had been replaced by a 21-element example with firebox shoulder washout doors but without extra washout plugs at the top of the first ring and the top feed cover was one of the later type usually fitted to domed boilers. The gangway doors were without rubber extensions, there was a train staff holder on the cab side, and a Mk 2 welded tender had replaced the original riveted Mk 1 in November 1945. Livery was plain black with yellow, shaded vermilion, 10in numerals and 14in tender letters. Note that although the train appears ready to depart, there were no lamps showing but a large 'K' had been chalked on the smokebox door.*                    AUTHORS' COLLECTION

## Transverse top feed cover

*This type of cover was intended for use on Type 3B boilers fitted with domes and went with the original style of top feed. Top feeds used on boilers built from 1947 onwards had both clack boxes incorporated directly into a redesigned casting with the setscrews projecting above the centre portion and protected by a fairing that stood proud of the main cover. Some of the earlier boilers were fitted with these top feeds, clacks and covers after about 1948. Although supposedly for use on domed boilers, the type of top feed cover shown here occasionally could be seen on domeless examples. Once again, this was particularly likely on locomotives stationed in Scotland.*

## Class 5 dome casing

*This drawing illustrates the dome casing that was used on either 24-element, vertical-throatplate or 28-element, sloping-throatplate Type 3B domed boilers.*

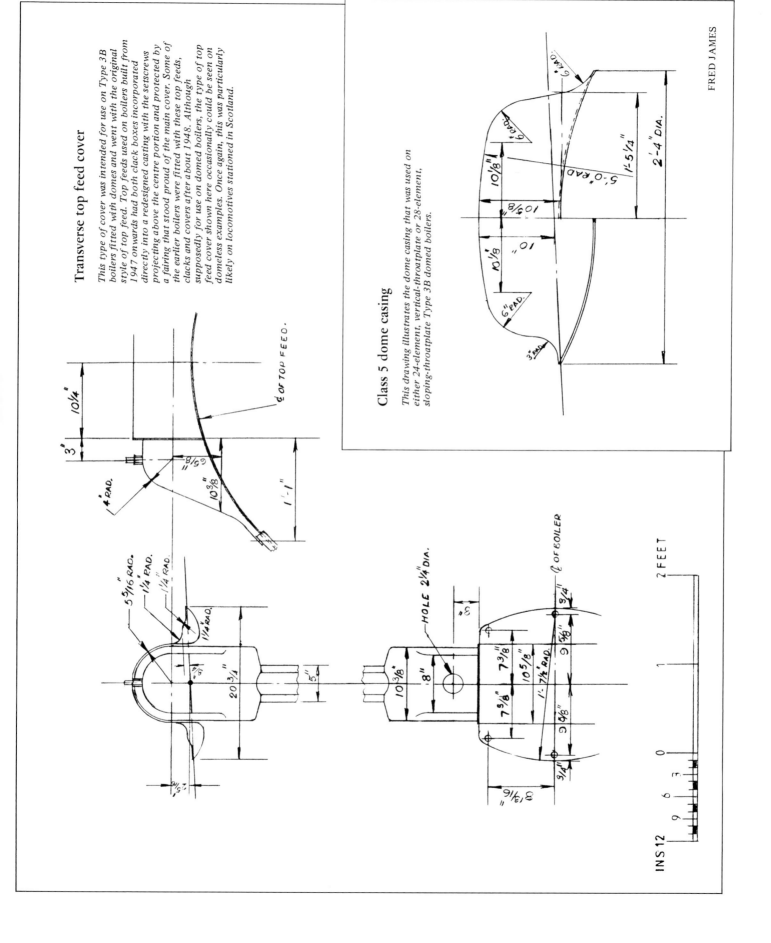

FRED JAMES

INS 12

*No. 45084 was built by the Vulcan Foundry in March 1935 and in the mid-1960s became the subject of this photograph, which illustrates a number of changes from its original condition. Countersunk rivets in the bufferbeam had been replaced by snap-head rivets and the beam was drilled to allow the fitting of a snowplough — note the two vertical rows of three holes set just inside the line of the frames. At some time, the engine had also been fitted with front steam heating, which it didn't have when built, as shown by the holes at the lower edge of the beam just inside those for the right-hand snowplough attachment. The guard for the AWS receiver can be seen below the beam and the locomotive's home depot, Stirling, was painted to the right of the coupling. The latter, together with the polished edge of the smokebox door number plate, show the engine to have been painted at St. Rollox. A support bracket had been fitted to the right-hand side of the door ring, together with a corresponding lug on the door, and the top lamp holder had been moved to the left-hand side. This, together with the warning flashes on the drop sections of the platform, was a result of overhead electrification. The steam lance cock is shown in the high position compared with that of 5005 on page 11.*

*There had been quite a few alterations to No. 45020, first of the Class 5s to enter service, since being built when it was photographed in the late 1950s. Its buffer beam had been repaired using shallow round-head rivets and a step had been fitted between the frames above the platform. A total of three access covers had appeared on each of its cylinder casings, the bracket supporting the fronts of the cylinder drain pipes had been removed and steam sanding was fitted in lieu of gravity sanding with hot-water de-sanding. Extra liner plates, a hinged cross bar, and support bracket for the door had been fitted to the smokebox, the tube cleaner cock had been moved higher up, and the original tall chimney had been replaced with one of standard height. Solid bogie axles had replaced the original, hollow, ones and the engine was carrying a sloping-throatplate, domed boiler. Although not visible, the crosshead vacuum pump would have been removed and the atomiser would have been mounted without a cover lower down on the smokebox side than originally positioned. The engine no longer had its original frames and had lost its makers' plates. Livery was lined black with Gill Sans smokebox door number plate.*
COLLECTION P. TATLOW

## CYLINDERS

Outside steam pipes between smokebox and cylinders were encased in sheet steel clothing with a roughly D-shaped cross-section. Where it joined the platform there were recesses both front and back of the clothing, those on the first ten Vulcan Foundry engines, Nos. 5020–5029, being considerably larger than the others. Although most of the casings with large recesses remained with their original loco-motives, some found their way on to others.

Cylinder clothing at first had no access holes or covers but on engines built after about June 1935 there were small circular plates secured by four screws. Earlier engines were then altered as they passed through the shops. After a few years, the holes and their covers were enlarged to almost twice the original size and by the mid-1940s all engines appear to have been modified. Two rectangular cover plates on the shoulders of the cylinder clothing were added from about 1937. Three copper drain pipes, clipped together at the front and supported by a bracket attached to the end cover, were fitted to each cylinder. After nationalisation many, though not all, engines lost the brackets and just had the ends of the pipes bound together.

*This close-up view shows the cylinder drains on No. 45121 after the retaining bracket originally fitted at the front had been removed in BR days. Enginemen called the cylinder drains 'the taps' and it was not unknown for them to stick in the partly open position, which meant a steady escape of steam and a series of hissing sounds when the loco-motive was running.*
HMRS (ACC312)

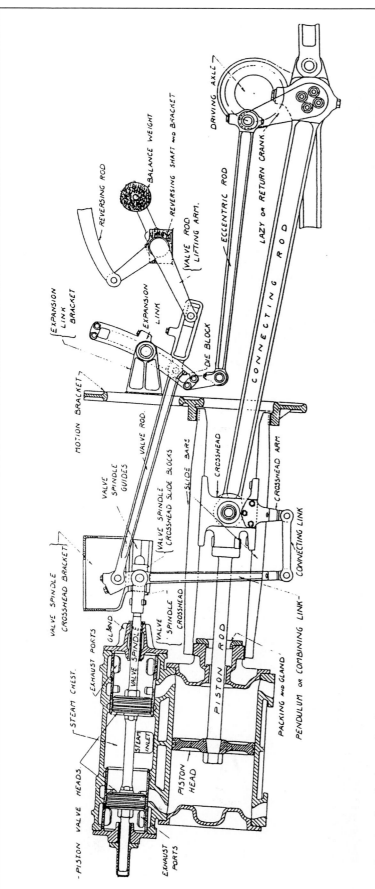

## Sketch of Walschaerts' valve gear

*Whilst not exactly the same as the Walschaerts' valve gear layout on a Class 5, this sketch has been included to help readers identify the various components referred to in the book. The main difference between what is shown here and a Class 5 was in the arrangement of the expansion link bearings. What is labelled in this drawing as the motion bracket was referred to on a Class 5 as the slidebar bracket and from it a girder bracket extended to a separate motion bracket to the rear. The expansion link bearings were mounted near to the middle of the girder bracket. What is shown here as the pendulum or combining link was also known as the combination lever, which is what we have called it in this book as well as in LMS Locomotive Profiles No. 5. Similarly, we have referred to what is here labelled as the connecting link by its alternative name of union link.*

## MOTION

Outside Walschaerts valve gear was fitted, that on Nos. 5000–5069 having the Horwich type of combination lever, which was of plain rectangular section and cranked below the valve spindle guide, whereas the remainder had a straight, fluted combination lever with a slight offset.

## FRAMES

Frames were only 1in thick and lightly stayed, all except the bogie stretcher being fabricated rather than cast. Problems with frame cracks led to later modifications and the springing arrangement was altered in 1951. Instead of spring hangers under compression, J brackets were added to the bottoms of the frames and tensioned hangers fitted. Early in 1943, a spare set of frames of the later type designed to accept sloping-throatplate boilers was made complete with cylinders, dragbox and stretchers. From then on, engines whose frames required more extensive repairs than usual received the spare set and their own became the spares after repair. Thus, frames from different manufacturers were exchanged between engines and, because most engines had the makers' plates on the frames, whereas the stock number went with the rest of the engine, this sometimes led to anomalies.

## WHEELS AND SANDING

The 6ft diameter coupled wheels had 19 spokes and Stanier's hallmark triangular-section rims. The first seventy locomotives had wheels with stiffening webs at the rear of the four spokes adjacent to the crankpins and the coupled axles originally fitted to all the engines were bored out. Later replacement wheels did not have the stiffening webs and replacement axles were solid. However, some of the locomotives that were built with stiffening webs had their original wheelsets replaced and these sets were subsequently used with other locomotives. One example of this practice known to us was No. 45150.

Balance weights shaped as truncated crescents were built up with steel plates riveted onto inside and outside faces of the wheels, those on leading and trailing wheels positioned opposite the crankpin and covering five spokes. Driving wheels had larger weights covering eight spokes displaced one spoke clockwise from a point opposite the crankpin. Rivets on the plates were originally countersunk and

*There had been quite a few alterations to No. 45020, first of the Class 5s to enter service, since being built when it was photographed in the late 1950s. Its buffer beam had been repaired using shallow round-head rivets and a step had been fitted between the frames above the platform. A total of three access covers had appeared on each of its cylinder casings, the bracket supporting the fronts of the cylinder drain pipes had been removed and steam sanding was fitted in lieu of gravity sanding with hot-water de-sanding. Extra liner plates, a hinged cross bar, and support bracket for the door had been fitted to the smokebox, the tube cleaner cock had been moved higher up, and the original tall chimney had been replaced with one of standard height. Solid bogie axles had replaced the original, hollow, ones and the engine was carrying a sloping-throatplate, domed boiler. Although not visible, the crosshead vacuum pump would have been removed and the atomiser would have been mounted without a cover lower down on the smokebox side than originally positioned. The engine no longer had its original frames and had lost its makers' plates. Livery was lined black with Gill Sans smokebox door number plate.*

COLLECTION P. TATLOW

## CYLINDERS

Outside steam pipes between smokebox and cylinders were encased in sheet steel clothing with a roughly D-shaped cross-section. Where it joined the platform there were recesses both front and back of the clothing, those on the first ten Vulcan Foundry engines, Nos. 5020–5029, being considerably larger than the others. Although most of the casings with large recesses remained with their original loco-motives, some found their way on to others.

Cylinder clothing at first had no access holes or covers but on engines built after about June 1935 there were small circular plates secured by four screws. Earlier engines were then altered as they passed through the shops. After a few years, the holes and their covers were enlarged to almost twice the original size and by the mid-1940s all engines appear to have been modified. Two rectangular cover plates on the shoulders of the cylinder clothing were added from about 1937. Three copper drain pipes, clipped together at the front and supported by a bracket attached to the end cover, were fitted to each cylinder. After nationalisation many, though not all, engines lost the brackets and just had the ends of the pipes bound together.

*This close-up view shows the cylinder drains on No. 45121 after the retaining bracket originally fitted at the front had been removed in BR days. Enginemen called the cylinder drains 'the taps' and it was not unknown for them to stick in the partly open position, which meant a steady escape of steam and a series of hissing sounds when the loco-motive was running.*

HMRS (ACC312)

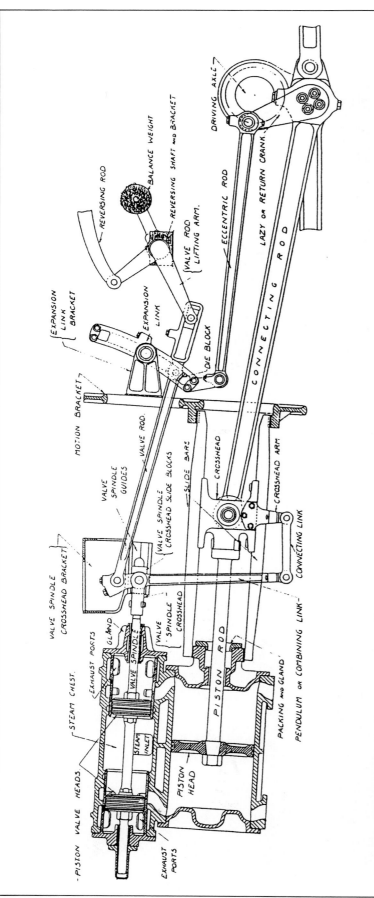

## Sketch of Walschaerts' valve gear

*Whilst not exactly the same as the Walschaerts' valve gear layout on a Class 5, this sketch has been included to help readers identify the various components referred to in the book. The main difference between what is shown here and a Class 5 was in the arrangement of the expansion link bearings. What is labelled in this drawing as the motion bracket was referred to on a Class 5 as the slidebar bracket and from it a girder bracket extended to a separate motion bracket to the rear. The expansion link bearings were mounted near to the middle of the girder bracket. What is shown here as the pendulum or combining link was also known as the combination lever, which is what we have called it in this book as well as in LMS Locomotive Profiles No. 5. Similarly, we have referred to what is here labelled as the connecting link by its alternative name of union link.*

Component labels in sketch: DRIVING AXLE; REVERSING SHAFT and BRACKET; BALANCE WEIGHT; REVERSING ROD; VALVE ROD LIFTING ARM; EXPANSION LINK BRACKET; EXPANSION LINK; ECCENTRIC ROD; LAZY or RETURN CRANK; CONNECTING ROD; DIE BLOCK; MOTION BRACKET; VALVE ROD; VALVE SPINDLE GUIDES; VALVE SPINDLE CROSSHEAD SLIDE BLOCKS; SLIDE BARS; CROSSHEAD; CROSSHEAD ARM; CONNECTING LINK; PENDULUM or COMBINING LINK; PACKING and GLAND; VALVE SPINDLE CROSSHEAD; VALVE SPINDLE CROSSHEAD BRACKET; VALVE SPINDLE; GLAND; PISTON ROD; PISTON HEAD; STEAM INLET; EXHAUST PORTS; STEAM CHEST; EXHAUST PORTS; PISTON VALVE HEADS

## MOTION

Outside Walschaerts valve gear was fitted, that on Nos. 5000–5069 having the Horwich type of combination lever, which was of plain rectangular section and cranked below the valve spindle guide, whereas the remainder had a straight, fluted combination lever with a slight offset.

## FRAMES

Frames were only 1in thick and lightly stayed, all except the bogie stretcher being fabricated rather than cast. Problems with frame cracks led to later modifications and the springing arrangement was altered in 1951. Instead of spring hangers under compression, J brackets were added to the bottoms of the frames and tensioned hangers fitted. Early in 1943, a spare set of frames of the later type designed to accept sloping-throatplate boilers was made complete with cylinders, dragbox and stretchers. From then on, engines whose frames required more extensive repairs than usual received the spare set and their own became the spares after repair. Thus, frames from different manufacturers were exchanged between engines and, because most engines had the makers' plates on the frames, whereas the stock number went with the rest of the engine, this sometimes led to anomalies.

## WHEELS AND SANDING

The 6ft diameter coupled wheels had 19 spokes and Stanier's hallmark triangular-section rims. The first seventy locomotives had wheels with stiffening webs at the rear of the four spokes adjacent to the crankpins and the coupled axles originally fitted to all the engines were bored out. Later replacement wheels did not have the stiffening webs and replacement axles were solid. However, some of the locomotives that were built with stiffening webs had their original wheelsets replaced and these sets were subsequently used with other locomotives. One example of this practice known to us was No. 45150.

Balance weights shaped as truncated crescents were built up with steel plates riveted onto inside and outside faces of the wheels, those on leading and trailing wheels positioned opposite the crankpin and covering five spokes. Driving wheels had larger weights covering eight spokes displaced one spoke clockwise from a point opposite the crankpin. Rivets on the plates were originally countersunk and

*Both these pictures show No. 5000 following preservation and restoration as part of the National Collection. The top picture clearly illustrates that whilst the leading and trailing coupled axles are hollow, the driving axle is solid with only a turning centre, and the original coupled wheels have been replaced by ones without stiffening webs to the spokes. Note the round-head rivets on the balance weights, steam sanding valve and drives from the rear of the expansion link to operate the mechanical lubricators. In the photograph above it can be seen that the cranked, plain section combination lever originally fitted to 5000 has been replaced by one of the later, fluted variety. We have mentioned elsewhere the problem of humping sand from the sand oven to the locomotive and then having to lift the heavy can onto the running plate before pouring sand into the fillers, the forward two of which on the right-hand side can be seen in this picture.*  AUTHORS' COLLECTION

*This view of the centre driving wheel shows the substantial nature of the coupling and connecting rods on the Class 5s. Note the four-stud fastening for the return crank and the solid axle with only a turning centre in the end; this was used to centre the wheelset when the tyres were being turned on a wheel lathe.*
AUTHORS' COLLECTION

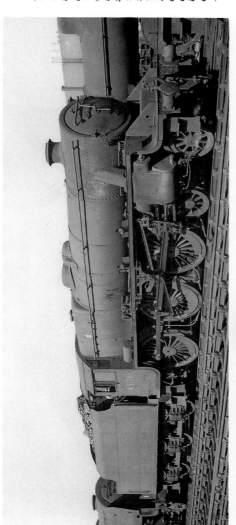

Another locomotive fitted with a 24-element, domed, vertical-throatplate boiler was Armstrong Whitworth-built 45176, seen in this view at Kingmoor in August 1962. It first received such a boiler in March 1954 but by March 1964 once more had a vertical throat-plate, domeless example. The blanking plates in the clothing show that it had previously carried a boiler with firebox shoulder wash-out doors. There were extra washout plugs at the front of the first ring, liner plates had been riveted inside the smokebox, and a door support bracket had been added to the front ring. The last point, together with the lack of liner plates at the front, would suggest that the engine may have received a new smokebox but we can't be sure. The frames still carried Armstrong Whitworth makers' plates and the buffer beam had been refitted using snap-head rivets. It had retained a riveted tender and the top feed cover was of the type fitted to domeless boilers. The engine was fitted with AWS. Although over-head electrification warning flashes had been applied, the smokebox door lamp holder was still in the upper position. Built in August 1935, the locomotive was withdrawn in August 1966. P. H. GROOM

After the spare set of frames was produced in 1943, exchanges as engines passed through the shops sometimes produced anomalies with makers' plates. Until seeing this photograph of 5154, however, we were unaware of the same situation arising through changes of smokeboxes. Armstrong Whitworth built the engine in June 1935 with that firm's rectangular plates on its front frames, which are still apparent in the photograph, but the smokebox bore Vulcan Foundry plates. This would indicate that it had changed smokeboxes, even though an engine normally retained its own smokebox when undergoing repair. The boiler was one of the 24-element, domed variety that was rebuilt from a 14-element, domeless one but was still without the extra washout plugs on the first barrel ring that were introduced in 1946. This, together with the fact that the tender was a riveted Mk 1, which type was recorded as coupled to 5154 from February 1942 to October 1946 and again from April 1947, suggests a date sometime in the mid-1940s. Lack of visible lining together with 10in scroll-and-serif yellow, shaded vermilion, numbers indicates wartime repainting. As well as the Vulcan Foundry plates, the smokebox had received long liner plates, as shown by the horizontal row of rivets above the steam pipe, and the firebox had blanking plates where holes had been cut previously for washout doors. Circular access covers in the cylinder clothing had been enlarged, the crosshead vacuum pump and hot-water de-sanding had been removed, and steam sanding had replaced the gravity sanding with which the engine was built. Balance weights on the coupled wheels were still flush-riveted. No. 5154 was named Lanarkshire Yeomanry in April 1937. R. K. BLENCOWE

flush but, following wartime and post-nationalisation repairs, some engines had partly countersunk, shallow round-head rivets on one or more wheelsets.

As built, all the engines had gravity, or trickle, sanding. There were six sand boxes, four in front of the leading and intermediate coupled wheels and two behind the latter. The four forward sand boxes were inside the frames with filler pipes reaching above the platform; the rear ones were outside the frames immediately below the platform. Filler lids were the later LMS pattern with concave tops and integrally cast handles.

The engines were built with hot-water de-sanding apparatus, which automatically directed a jet of hot water onto the rails when sanding was applied. This worked when the locomotive was running either engine or tender first. The water pipes were clipped to the leading sand pipes whilst at the other end they were attached to brackets suspended from the frames.

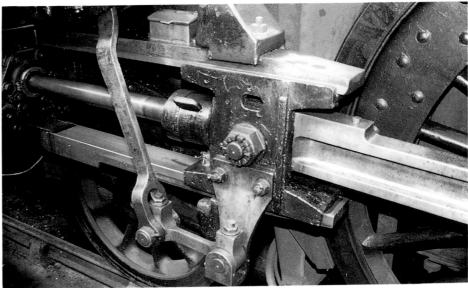

*Although this view of the left-hand slide bars and crosshead on No. 45025 shows the original style of cranked combination lever, the original crosshead with bolt holes for attaching the drive to a vacuum pump had been replaced and round-head rivets had been used to repair the coupled wheel balance weight. The brass oil box on top of the upper slide bar was for crosshead lubrication.*
D. P. ROWLAND

*The later type of fluted combination lever fitted to Nos. 5070 et seq when built and used when replacements were required for earlier engines is seen in this view of No. 45121. Although the locomotive was built with solid axles to both its bogie wheelsets, the leading one had been replaced by a hollow example when this picture was taken. The crosshead had been replaced, round-head rivets had been used on the balance weight, and AWS had been fitted, as witnessed by the electrical conduit clipped to the platform angle. Note the circular and rectangular access covers in the cylinder clothing.*
HMRS (ACC311)

*Recesses in the outside steam pipe casings were longer than usual on the first ten Vulcan Foundry engines, an example of which is shown in this view of 5021 at Perth in May 1935. The tall chimney and external feed pipes peculiar to the Vulcan Foundry are also evident, as is the bracket attached to the bottom of the cylinder front cover supporting the front ends of the drain pipes. The engine's buffer beam had been drilled for mounting a snow plough and a step plate had been fitted between the front frames by the time this picture was taken but the cab was still without rain gutters. The fitting near the front of the smokebox wrapper just above the saddle was the tube cleaner cock. Note the stiffening webs at the rear of the four spokes adjacent to the crankpins, the hollow bogie axles and the plain tender axlebox covers.*

AUTHORS' COLLECTION

Between 1938 and 1948, steam sanding was fitted and the hot-water de-sanding apparatus removed. The visible differences between trickle and steam sanding can be seen in some of the photographs.

## BRAKES

A combined large and small ejector was mounted alongside the boiler in front of the left-hand side of the cab and a crosshead-driven vacuum pump was fixed below the bottom left-hand slidebar. The brackets attaching the pump to the slide-bars on early Crewe and Vulcan Foundry engines had gusset plates between the end castings whereas the others didn't. From 1938, the pumps were removed.

## BOGIE

A De Glehn-type side control bolster bogie with Derby-style frames was used. Wheels had ten spokes and triangular-

*This undated picture shows No. 5000 when it still had a vacuum pump, stiffening webs at the rear of some of its coupled wheel spokes, flush-riveted balance weights, plain section, cranked combination levers and gravity sanding.* AUTHORS' COLLECTION

*Whilst showing No. 45110 as preserved during the 1980s, this photograph was taken before the locomotive was completely dismantled and rebuilt in the early 1990s. The electrical conduit clipped to the edge of the platform angle and the small timing reservoir just ahead of the cab were both features of AWS that had been fitted to the locomotive in May 1959. The triangular rim of the coupled wheels, designed to stiffen them and prevent flexure between spoke ends, is apparent as is the hollow axle. The sanding valve and nearly horizontal lower end of the rear sanding pipe, both characteristic of steam sanding, are obvious. The small tube at bottom left of the picture between coupling rod and sand pipe was a late alteration and was the socket for inserting a lever to rock the ashpan and so empty it over a pit.* AUTHORS' COLLECTION

Sloping-throatplate boilers had the firebox tubeplate further forward, which can be seen in this photograph of 45109 taken at Willesden during the first half of 1959 before it was fitted with AWS in June of that year. It was first fitted with a sloping-throatplate, domed boiler in May 1948 and retained the type until withdrawal in April 1967. Although round-head rivets had been used when repairing the coupled wheel balance weights, the axles were still hollow. There was no longer a bracket supporting the fronts of the cylinder drain pipes. Livery was typical of a locomotive repainted in England with 8in numbers in line with the tender emblem and lined cylinder clothing bands.
AUTHORS' COLLECTION

section rims and bogie axles on the first fifty Vulcan Foundry engines, Nos. 5020–5069, and Crewe-built Nos. 5000–5003 were hollow; those on the rest were solid. Replacement axles were solid and engines were sometimes seen with one solid and one hollow example.

## PLATFORM AND BUFFER BEAM

The platform narrowed at the drop section and was reinforced along the lower edge by angle-iron. The buffer beam narrowed below the level of the angle and was flush-riveted on Crewe-built engines. Vulcan Foundry and Armstrong Whitworth locomotives had two round-head rivets at each end. Later repairs at Crewe continued to use flush rivets on the beams whereas other works often used round-head ones. After nationalisation, round-head rivets became more common.

Locomotives built at Crewe each had a front steam-heating valve and pipe fixed to the bottom edge of the buffer beam just to the right of the vacuum pipe dummy but those built by outside contractors, i.e., Nos. 5020–5069 and 5075–5224, did not. Some of the latter, however, were later fitted with them.

All Crewe and Armstrong Whitworth-built engines, as well as Vulcan Foundry examples from 5045 onwards, were built with a raised step between the frames in front of the smokebox saddle. The first 25 Vulcan Foundry engines did not have these steps when built but were fitted with them by the late 1930s.

## CAB

Nos. 5020–5069 were built without rain gutters at the edges of the roof but were fitted with them later, whereas Nos. 5000–5019 and 5070 et seq had gutters from new. Inside, a toolbox with an oak lid that formed a seat was fitted on the right-hand side and a tip-up oak seat for the driver attached to the left-hand cab side. On at least some engines, the toolbox was later moved forward and a tip-up seat like that on the driver's side was fitted on the right. Folding gangway doors had rubber sheet extensions at the bottom, which in later years were often omitted. Front windows originally had spring-loaded catches but they were replaced after about 1938 by rotating handles and catches. From about 1955, some engines received hinged armrests that could be folded out over the cab window runners when the rear windows were open.

*We know of forty-six locomotives that were fitted with BTH speed indicators between February 1938 and February 1944, although by the end of World War Two all the equipment had been removed. One of the earliest locomotives to be modified was 5042, which received a speed indicator in June 1938 and is seen with it in this photograph taken soon afterwards. The long bracket to which the alternator was attached can be seen underneath the platform just ahead of the cab. Built by the Vulcan Foundry in October 1934, the engine still had its original smokebox with makers' plates on the sides and tall chimney but had been fitted with a 24-element, domed boiler rebuilt from one of the 14-element, domeless ones first used on 5000-5006 and 5020-5069. The locomotive received this boiler in May 1938 and, since its previous boiler did not have firebox shoulder washout doors, there were no blanking plates in the firebox clothing. Bogie axles were still hollow and the engine was still equipped with gravity sanding and hot-water de-sanding but the vacuum pump had been removed. Coupled wheels had stiffening webs behind the spokes adjacent to the crank pins, balance weights were flush-riveted and tender axlebox covers were plain. Both circular and rectangular access covers had been fitted to the cylinder clothing and rain gutters added to the sides of the roof. Livery was 1936 block style.*     AUTHORS' COLLECTION

Some engines were fitted with automatic tablet exchange apparatus outside the cab on the left hand side; these fittings are described further on page 9. It was fixed near the back of the cab on the left-hand side at footplate height. Some locomotives used on single-line routes that employed train staffs had holders fitted to the cab sides about a foot below the windows. When locomotives were transferred to other districts and did not require tablet exchange apparatus it was removed and the equipment retained at the depot for further use.

## SPEED INDICATORS AND AWS

Between 1938 and 1943, some locomotives were fitted with British Thompson Houston speed recorders. The alternator was mounted on a bracket suspended from the platform alongside the left-hand trailing wheel and driven by a pin on the end of a small return crank from the driving wheel crankpin. The equipment was removed in 1944. Between 1959 and 1964, a few engines received Smith-Stone speed indicators, the alternators for which were mounted directly on to the return cranks. Details of the engines involved are in the *Profile*.

From 1959, most of this series were fitted with the BR Automatic Warning

System (AWS), which was also sometimes known as Automatic Train Control (ATC). They had an extra frame stretcher at the front of the bogie to which the AWS receiver was fixed and had a guard plate attached to the buffer beam. An electrical conduit ran along the left-hand platform

angle, the main vacuum reservoir was immediately in front of the cab on the right-hand platform, and the smaller timing reservoir was on the left. Locomotives we known to have been fitted with BR AWS are listed in *LMS Locomotive Profile No. 5*.

*Among the thirteen locomotives we know to have been fitted with Smith-Stone speed recorders in the 1960s was 45040, which received the equipment in April 1963. This photograph, taken at Tyseley in November 1964, shows that, unlike on the BTH installation, the alternator was mounted directly onto a return crank from the trailing crankpin. At the time the engine was stationed at Saltley, as shown by the 2E shed code painted on the smokebox door where its previous 21A plate had been when shed codes were changed. It was fitted with a sloping-throatplate, domed boiler – a type it first received in November 1936 – and the top feed cover was the later, postwar, pattern with a raised fairing over the centrally mounted clack set-screws. Both bogie axles and the driving axle had been replaced by solid ones but leading and trailing coupled axles were still hollow. Driving wheel balance weights were still flush-riveted whereas those on the leading and trailing wheels had round-head rivets and there were no support brackets to the cylinder drain pipes. The smokebox had front and side liner plates but retained a fixed crossbar and the top lamp holder had been moved to the left-hand side of the door. The leading and intermediate axlebox covers on the Mk 1 riveted tender had cruciform ribs cast in whereas the trailing one was still plain. A close study reveals that there was actually lining underneath the grime and that the tender wore post-1956 heraldic crests.*     T. J. EDGINGTON

*Although this tender actually ran behind a rebuilt 'Royal Scot', it differed in only a few respects from those paired with Class 5s. The main difference was in the depth of the front footplate supports, which was necessitated by the greater height of the cab floor on a 'Scot' and meant that the fireman had to bend further in order to shovel coal. The other notable difference is more difficult to detect and is only evident from the small cast-iron label on the tender front partially hidden by the brake handle. This reads 'TENDER BRAKED TO SUIT 250 LBS PRESS' and was fitted after November 1937 when all tenders were checked to ensure that the sleeving of the brake cylinders was suited to the boiler pressure of the engines to which they were attached. On tenders coupled to Class 5s, the label would have indicated 225 lbs as the suitable pressure. Below the pressure label can be seen the water valve handle to the exhaust injector and the indicating plaque reading from top to bottom 'SHUT WATER OPEN' whilst at the other side of the shovelling plate the live steam injector water valve handle and indicator plaque are evident. Beyond that was the water scoop operating handle with its associated indicator rod and plaque reading from top to bottom 'OUT SCOOP IN' but apparently lacking a securing chain. Outside the plaque, the bracket bolted to the tender front adjacent to the side plate was for holding the gangway door closed. As can be seen, the coal space door could fold in the middle, the two halves being held in line by locking bars. Although the Stanier tenders were designed to be self-trimming, in practice the fireman would have to open the doors and go into the coal space once he had used the coal immediately to the front and dislodge more with either the coal pick or firing shovel. Next to the coal space doors was the enginemen's locker whilst, although not visible in this view, between locker and tender side was a water gauge and lamp holder for stowing the driver's hand lamp or a spare headlamp. On the opposite, fireman's side of the tender front can be seen the tunnel that extended into the tank and normally held a clinker shovel, straight dart and rake. Because the working ends of these fire irons could not be seen when they were stowed, the end shapes of the handles identified them — round for the clinker shovel, triangular for the rake and oval for the dart. The coal pick would be carried either on top of the housing for the coal doors or where the cloth can be seen by the handbrake. Next to the tunnel were two holders for locomotive headlamps, the projection above the top one being primarily to protect the lamps from falling coal but often used as a step for access to the coal space when the doors were not open.*

AUTHORS' COLLECTION

# TENDER VARIATIONS

*Locomotives built at Crewe Works and by the Vulcan Foundry were coupled when new to Mk 1 tenders having riveted tanks. Such a tender, No. 9056, is seen in this view of engine No. 5003, which was built at Crewe in March 1935. The first Vulcan Foundry tenders had short vents but by the time 9056 was built, the vents had been extended to the height shown here and earlier ones had been altered. Vulcan Foundry tenders were also slightly different from all others in that the axlebox covers were plain rather than having the cruciform ribs cast into them that are apparent in this photograph. The locomotive seems to have been in original condition and was one of four Crewe examples fitted with hollow bogie axles.*
AUTHORS' COLLECTION

The Vulcan Foundry locomotives and all but three of the Crewe Works engines were coupled to standard Mark I, or Type I, tenders having 7ft 6in + 7ft 6in wheelbase with 4ft 3in diameter, triangular-section rim wheels. The first fifty Vulcan Foundry-built tenders attached initially to 5050–5069 had flat outside faces to the axlebox covers. All others had covers with cruciform ribs cast in to them, which type was also used on the earlier tenders when replacements were required.

All tenders were fitted with steam heating pipes, valves, standpipes and hoses, the latter being mounted at the bottom edge of the buffer beam just to the left of the coupling hook. The equipment was only fitted during the colder months when there was an operating requirement to heat the carriages of passenger trains, and in warmer weather it was removed for storage and possibly overhaul. Each year the dates that steam heating was to commence and cease, together with any other instructions that might apply, were circulated to members of staff well in advance so that equipment could be fitted to or removed from locomotives.

The footplate was raised above the frames to match the height of the cab floor

*No. 5143/45143 was coupled throughout its life from June 1935 to December 1965 to Mk 2 welded tenders like the one seen in this photograph taken at Chester in November 1964. Apart from the lack of rivet heads, there was no external difference between any of the Mk 1 or Mk 2 tenders coupled to Class 5s apart from the variations in axlebox covers referred to earlier and a brief period when short vents were used. This one shows the cruciform ribbed type of axlebox cover that constituted the majority. Note the steam-heating hose, with which all Class 5 tenders were equipped, and the overhead electrification warning flashes that were applied after 1960. No. 45143 was painted at St. Rollox in fully-lined livery with 10in Gill Sans cabside numerals mounted relatively low down and the power classification figures above them. The tender carried the post-1956 BR crests, that on the right-hand side being the corrected version with a left-facing lion, and although the rectangular number plate is evident, there was no capacity plate.*
AUTHORS' COLLECTION

*Problems were encountered with the welded tanks on Mk 2 tenders leaking and so a part-welded version was introduced. Somewhat confusingly, these tenders were also referred to as Mk 1s and whilst none of the first 225 Class 5s ran with them from new, some were coupled to them at various times in later years. This photograph of No. 45168, originally paired with a Mk 2 welded tender, shows it coupled to a part-welded Mk 1 at Craigentinny in August 1956. It first ran with this type of tender between April 1950 and February 1951 but we don't know when it acquired the one seen here. Apart from having fewer rivets visible, part-welded tenders had different vents from others with a rectangular cross-section attached directly to the rear coal plate. Some later examples also had roller bearings and external sieve boxes, neither of which was fitted to this one. The locomotive was in typical St. Rollox livery with 10in cabside numerals and was fitted with a train staff holder for use on single-line sections.*
AUTHORS' COLLECTION

*This picture of Mk 1 tender No. 9174, taken at Holbeck in June 1966 when it was coupled to No. 45079, shows the left-hand leading axlebox with cruciform ribs cast into its cover, this particular tender having been so equipped from new, as well as the type of spring associated with these axle-boxes. This arrangement pertained to the vast majority of 4,000 gallon tenders until well after nationalisation. Whilst platforms and steps on engines and tenders were in line when built, different amounts of wear on tyres and springs, as well as setting of the latter, could later result in the sort of misalignment seen here. Also visible is the fall plate between the cab floor and front platform of the tender and the gangway door. Note that the latter was without the rubber extension that was originally attached to the lower edge. The difference in positioning and fixing of the lower extremities of the locomotive and tender commode handrails, often known to enginemen as 'uprights', is evident. Those on the engine were mounted on the wing plates rather than cab sides due to loading gauge restrictions. The live steam injector overflow pipe can be seen attached to the under-side of the lower cab footstep.*
AUTHORS' COLLECTION

*This picture shows the rivet pattern on the side of the tender, which differed slightly from the three rebuilt Pacific tenders where the side plate was riveted to the top of the front bulkhead. The rebuilt tenders also had a different profile at the top rear that brought the last double, vertical row of rivets closer to the edge of the plate.* AUTHORS' COLLECTION

*This picture illustrates the inward curve of the side plate that was incorporated in order to allow fitting of the commode-style handrail within the loading gauge. When the first Mk 1 tenders were built, there were lockers either side of the coal space access doors but later examples had only one locker, as seen here with the door standing open. When the door was closed, a hasp could be folded over the tongue seen on the side of the locker just above the beading and a pin on the end of the chain hanging from just above it dropped through the hole to keep the door shut. The two brackets near the bottom of the locker door were meant to secure a block of wood that held spare water gauge glasses but in the final years of steam maintenance standards fell and the block of wood had been removed when this picture was taken. In such circumstances, it was common practice for the driver and/or fireman to carry a spare water gauge glass. Below the locker door can be seen part of the water scoop operating handle that was secured by a chain to prevent inadvertent lowering should it, for instance, be mistaken for the brake handle that is clearly visible on the other side of the tender. Lowering of the scoop if the tender was traversing pointwork or crossings could have serious consequences. Just above the loose coal on the tender footplate is the shovelling plate that was positioned several inches above it in order to make life easier for the fireman when shovelling coal into the firebox.* AUTHORS' COLLECTION

*Evident in this view are details of the tender rear such as the handrail used in conjunction with the rear side footsteps and the three steps on the back plate for access to the water filler. Adjacent to the vacuum hose is the oval 4,000 gallon water capacity plate and above it can be seen the rectangular tender number plate. At the end of the chain hanging from the vacuum hose, or end train pipe as it was sometimes known, was a pin not visible in this picture that was used to lock the hose either to its dummy or to the brake hose of another locomotive or vehicle to which it was coupled. The four pieces of angle-iron riveted to the platform and back plate were to secure the tank and were present on all types of Class 5 tender, although on welded and part-welded versions they were welded to the back plate whilst still riveted to the platform. Just inside the top footsteps can be seen a pair of very grubby overhead electrification warning flashes.* AUTHORS' COLLECTION

*This picture shows details of the left-hand rear footsteps and support plate, steam-heating hose and securing chain on a Mk 1 Stanier 4,000 gallon tender.* AUTHORS' COLLECTION

*The first three tenders made for 4—6—2s Nos. 6200-6203, one of which actually ran with* Royal Scot *on its tour of America, were rebuilt to be closely similar to standard Stanier Mk 1 tenders. One of them, No. 9002, was then coupled to Class 5 No. 5000 when that engine was built in 1935. The combination is seen in this view taken at Crewe South in September 1937 when both engine and tender were in fairly grubby condition. The visible differences from standard Mk 1s were that the curve of the sides above the rear of the tank was shallower and the rivet pattern was curved above the tank front. There were internal differences but they aren't apparent from outside. Two of the rebuilt tenders, Nos. 9000 and 9002, also differed in that they had roller bearing axleboxes, the distinctive covers of which are apparent in this picture. Note the hollow bogie axles, stiffening webs behind some of the coupled wheel spokes, and gravity sanding fitted to the engine.*                          W. L. GOOD

and there was a folding door in a housing projecting forward from the front plate for access to the coal space. Initially, lockers were provided either side of the coal space door but later only a single, albeit enlarged, locker was fitted on the left-hand side.

At first, the tank vent pipes mounted on the rear platform behind the coal fender were quite short, reaching only just above the level of the tank rear. Soon after the first tenders were built they were extended to the tops of the side plates.

Tanks on the Mk. I tenders were assembled with snap-head rivets. The second Armstrong Whitworth batch originally

*These two pictures show the top of the tank behind the rear coal plate. The large dome was positioned over the opening at the top of the water scoop and was designed to allow the pressure of water entering the tank to be dissipated and to fill the tank from above. The lid with a handle on top covered the filler used when taking water from a water crane or column and the tall vent pipes at either side were to allow air to escape as the tank filled. These vents were as seen here on riveted or welded tanks — on part-welded ones they were rectangular and mounted against the rear coal plate.*

**AUTHORS' COLLECTION**

coupled to Nos. 5125–5224, however, had tanks of welded construction and were known as the Mk. 2 or Type 2. Later still, a part-welded type, also called a Mk. 1, appeared and several ended up behind engines in the 5000–5224 series at various times.

The first three tenders coupled to 4–6–2s Nos. 6200–6202, numbered 9000–9002, were replaced in 1935 and rebuilt as Mk. 1s, although the curve at the top of the side plates differed slightly at the rear, their tank construction was somewhat different, and the rivet pattern on the sides was slightly different at the front. Nos. 9000 and 9002 had Timken roller bearing axleboxes. Once rebuilt, they were coupled to Class 5s Nos. 5073, 5074 and 5000 respectively but later appeared behind other engines in the class.

Two other tenders were attached to early Class 5s – a 3,500 gallon test tender built in 1937 and a coal weighing tender in the 1960s. Construction and modification details of Mk. 1 tenders as well as a table showing which type of tender was coupled to which locomotive and when can be found in *LMS Locomotive Profile No. 5.*

*From 1st December 1963 to 25th January 1965, No. 45081 was coupled to one of the four coal-weighing tenders, No. 10590, built for trials involving coal consumption calculations. This photograph was taken at Carlisle Upperby in November 1964 and shows not only the unusual tender pairing but also that the top feed cover on 45081's 24-element, vertical-throatplate, domed boiler was one of the round type normally only seen on vertical-throatplate boilers. Although the subject of coal-weighing tenders will be addressed in more detail in a subsequent volume, we have included this picture to illustrate the only occasion we know of when one of them was coupled to a Class 5 in the 5000-5224 series.*
AUTHORS' COLLECTION

*Under normal conditions it is almost impossible to photograph the underside of tender frames but when those frames are being repaired it is a different matter. This photograph was taken at the Midland Railway Centre in 2000 and shows the frames of a 4,000 gallon Stanier tender upside-down with the front nearest the camera. Although actually from a Mk 2 welded example, the frames can be taken as representative of any Mk 1 or Mk 2 tender. The drawbar and safety links had been removed but the intermediate buffers were still in situ. Between the forward lower extremities of the frames (actually at the top in this view) can be seen the brake gear weighshaft with fittings near either end to which the brake rodding would be attached. At the far end is the crank to which the hand brake rigging would be connected whilst between the two inner bearings is the large crank projecting rearwards to the steam cylinder. The leading horn guide nearest to the camera had been removed, as had the water pick-up operating gear and brake rodding. The triangular plates attached to what was actually the top of the frames, albeit at the bottom as shown here, were to support the tank.*
AUTHORS' COLLECTION

# COMPARISONS AND CONTRASTS

In the Introduction we used a number of pictures to illustrate some examples of the various production batches built at Crewe and by the two outside contractors, Vulcan Foundry and Armstrong Whitworth. In this section we have featured three locomotives that were all built in 1935 by the same

builder and show some of the variations that could be seen over the years.

As they passed through the workshops, locomotives built to the same order or lot number soon began to display a number of variations, some of which were quite subtle while others were strikingly obvious. We

believe that three photographs on these pages and others on pages 36–39 will make this point and will also provide readers with an idea of some details to look for when studying pictures of the class.

*All three engines featured in the photographs on these two pages were built by Armstrong Whitworth between July and September 1935 and were identical when first in service, their boilers being 21-element, vertical-throatplate types with firebox shoulder washout doors. No. 45163 was photographed at Balornock in June 1961 carrying a sloping-throatplate boiler with its top feed on the second ring. The smokebox had been fitted with an extra liner plate forward of the steam pipe, as shown by the horizontal row of rivets below the handrail, and a door support bracket. It did not, however, have any extra liner plate at the front under the smokebox door, evidenced by the lack of rivets on the door ring, nor did it have a hinged crossbar, which would have been shown by parallel rows of rivets halfway up the front of the wrapper. Its buffer beam had been repaired using flush rivets at the ends rather than the round-head ones with which it was built and had been drilled for the attachment of a snow plough. Both round and rectangular access covers had been fitted to the cylinder clothing, round-head rivets had been used in repairing all the coupled wheel balance weights, steam sanding had been fitted and hot-water de-sanding removed. AWS was fitted and the engine was coupled to a part-welded Mk 1 tender without roller bearings or external sieve boxes. The locomotive was fully lined except for the cylinder clothing bands and 8in Gill Sans cabside numerals were set low down with 5MT power classification above. The tender carried post-1956 crests with a heraldically correct left-facing lion on the right-hand side.*

*In contrast to 45163, No. 45177 is seen with a different version of the sloping-throatplate type 3B boiler having the top feed on its first*

*ring. The top feed was one of the type made from 1947 onwards in which both clack boxes were incorporated in a single casting, the setscrews being protected by a fairing that stood proud of the main cover. The buffer beam and smokebox were in the same state as those on 45163 and it had the same alterations to its cylinder clothing, balance weights and sanding. The engine was not fitted with AWS, although it received the equipment before withdrawal in July 1966, and it was coupled to a Mk 2 welded tender. Cabside numerals were 10in Gill Sans with 5MT power class above, the cylinder clothing bands had red lining and the tender had the pre-1956 BR lion-on-wheel emblems.*

*The third of the Armstrong Whitworth trio, No. 45178, was photographed at Balornock in November 1952. This engine retained its original type of vertical-throatplate, domeless boiler throughout its life, the only alteration apparent being the addition of two washout plugs on top of the first barrel ring just behind the smokebox. The smokebox itself had been fitted with longer side liner plates than those seen on 45163 and 45177 and rivets around the bottom of the door ring show that one had been fitted at the front. Buffer beam, balance weights and sanding were to the same pattern as 45163 and 45177 but the driving axle was solid. Although the picture was taken before Class 5s were fitted with AWS, 45178 did not, as far as we are aware, ever receive it. The tender to which it was coupled was a riveted Mk 1 that it received sometime after November 1949. Livery was similar to 45178's but the cabside numbers were spaced further apart and the power classification was simply '5' displayed below them.*

AUTHORS' COLLECTION and R. K. BLENCOWE

*This view of 5032 shows quite clearly the lack of rain gutters at the edges of the cab roof on the first fifty Vulcan Foundry locomotives. It also illustrates the left-hand hot-water de-sanding pipe attached to a bracket behind the trailing coupled wheel and the stiffening webs behind the coupled wheel spokes adjacent to the crankpins. Characteristics of the first fifty Vulcan Foundry engines, such as external steam pipes, tall chimney and hollow bogie axles, are evident. Note also the small recess in the steam pipe clothing just above the platform, gusset plate on the vacuum pump attachments, plain section, cranked combination lever and lack of access covers in the cylinder clothing. The shape of the sanding pipe behind the driving wheel and lack of steam valve immediately below the sand box are indications that gravity sanding was fitted. The curved extension at the bottom of the gangway door was a rubber sheet designed to help prevent draughts entering and lumps of coal falling off the footplate.*                                                   AUTHORS' COLLECTION

These three photographs show some of the changes made to Armstrong Whitworth No. 5151 between its entering service in November 1934 and withdrawal in November 1966. Here it is seen at Carstairs in April 1939 carrying its original type of 21-element, vertical-throatplate boiler without washout plugs on the first ring. Apart from round-head rivets on the driving wheel balance weight, the engine appears to have been unaltered since being built and was still fitted with gravity sanding and hot-water de-sanding apparatus. This picture shows 10in numbers on the cabside whilst the two BR era pictures opposite show variations in the positioning of numbers and power classification on the cab sides.
A. G. ELLIS

No. 5151 at Balornock in October 1951 after being renumbered as 45151 and receiving a sloping-throatplate boiler with top feed on the second ring and extra washout plugs on the first ring. The smokebox had been fitted with extra longitudinal liner plates, as shown by the horizontal row of rivets above the steam pipe, and the atomiser cock was in the lower position without a cover. A blanking plate had been fitted to the smokebox where the cock had originally been sited. Steam sanding had been fitted, hot-water de-sanding apparatus removed, and the engine was coupled to a Mk 1 part-welded tender.
AUTHORS' COLLECTION

No. 45151 is seen here in about 1959 or 1960 fitted with the sloping-throatplate boiler having its top feed on the first ring that it carried from March 1957 until withdrawal. Unusually, the top feed cover was one of the large, rounded pattern, normally only seen on vertical-throatplate, domeless boilers. Engine and Mk 2 welded tender were immaculately turned out in lined livery with 10in Gill Sans cabside numerals and pre-1956 lion-on-wheel emblems. The front axlebox cover on the tender was one of the plain-fronted ones originally fitted to Vulcan Foundry tenders coupled to Nos. 5020-5069 when built.
AUTHORS' COLLECTION

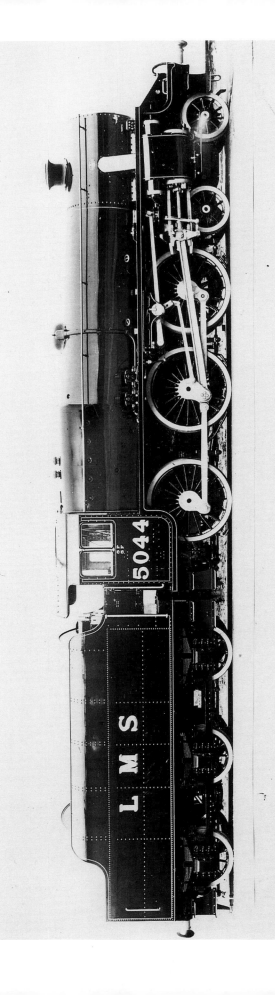

As can be seen in this study of Vulcan Foundry No. 5044, lining was applied to the rear of the boiler clothing band next to the smokebox and front of the angle between firebox clothing and cab front. It was also on the front and lower edges of the platform angles, inset from the edges of the cab sides, the inside edges of cylinder clothing bands, and inset from the edges of tender tank side and back plates. Contractor-built engines had the cabside lining continued around the windows, as can clearly be seen here, but Crewe Works stopped it at the eaves. Letters on the tender sides were 14in transfers spaced at 40in centres on Vulcan Foundry engines up to No. 5111 and Armstrong Whitworth examples to 5136 or 5137. The rest had 60in spacing. Stock numbers were 12in transfers, normally positioned as shown here, and the power classification was '5P' immediately below the cab windows with '5F' underneath it. Locomotive and tender were brand new when the picture was taken with hollow bogie axles, top feed pipes proud of the boiler clothing and plain tender axlebox covers.

F. MOORE

# LIVERY DETAILS

When the first Class 5s entered service in 1934 the official painting style for mixed traffic locomotives was often referred to as the 'Intermediate Passenger Livery'. Locomotive and tender were finished in varnished black, with a ⅜in wide vermilion line inset an inch from the front and lower edges of the platform angles, 2½in from the edges of the cab sides, on the inside edges of cylinder clothing bands, and inset 2in from the edges of tender tank side and back plates. The boiler clothing band next to the smokebox had a ½in vermilion line around the rear edge and the angle between firebox clothing and cab front had one around the front edge. Cab side lining varied somewhat between batches of engines as shown in the pictures. All of the first 225 Class 5s were painted when new in this style and had scroll & serif gold,

*Vulcan Foundry and Armstrong Whitworth engines had bright metal smokebox hinges, straps and darts when delivered and some locomotives had the tops of their frames polished at their home sheds. As this picture illustrates, however, some appear later to have had those items painted white, others we know of being 5055 and 5181. The locomotive was in standard condition for an Armstrong Whitworth product as built and carried a 21-element, domeless boiler. No. 5130 was stationed at 7A Llandudno Junction and was in charge of an express passenger train when photographed at Crewe.* AUTHORS' COLLECTION

*Whilst many of the later Class 5s were turned out with the shortlived 1936 block-style characters when new, we know of only thirty-five engines in the 5000-5224 series that received them when repainted. One was No. 5131 from 3E Monument Lane, seen here being prepared for duty at Crewe North with the driver's oil can standing on the top of its coupling rod. Numerals were 10in high and letters 14in, both being shaded vermilion, with letter spacing invariably 60in. Sans serif smokebox door plates were designed to match the transfers but, as far as we are aware, all repainted engines in the 5000-5224 series retained scroll-and-serif ones. Built by Armstrong Whitworth in May 1935, the engine received its first domed boiler – a 24-element rebuild of one of the original 14-element units – in August 1938, which is probably when this picture was taken. The smaller cover over the atomiser cock on engines with domed boilers can be seen and it will be noticed that at this time there were no washout plugs at the front of the first barrel ring. The locomotive and tender appear to have been freshly painted, which is to be expected as it had just undergone its first general repair, suggesting that stocks of the 1936 transfers were still being used up even though they had been superseded by new scroll-and-serif types. Note that although there were no washout doors on the firebox shoulders, there were no blanking plates either, which is not what we would expect as 5131 was originally built with a 21-element boiler that had shoulder washout doors. Thus, it would seem that the firebox clothing was either new or originally fitted to another locomotive. As well as the small circular access cover in the cylinder clothing with which it had been built, rectangular ones had been added to the shoulders and the crosshead vacuum pump had been removed. No. 5131 was the first Armstrong Whitworth engine to be built with its makers' plates on the frames – the left-hand one is just visible behind the lamp.* L. HANSON

In 1946, the LMS introduced a new style of block characters in straw colour with maroon edging and inset lining. They were usually applied to new locomotives but there were instances of repainted engines receiving them. The numbers came in two sizes – 10in and 12in – and we know of eight Class 5s in the 5000-5224 series that had the former and sixteen the latter. All were plain black and had the numbers placed immediately under the cab windows with a single, small power class figure '5' below. No. 5050 was photographed at Carnforth in May 1948 with 12in numbers and a 21-element, vertical-throatplate, domed boiler that had been fitted six months earlier. As with 5131, there is no evidence of blanking plates on the firebox shoulders, which suggests that the clothing was either new or from another engine. The smokebox had been fitted with short liner plates at the side, shown by the horizontal row of rivets above the steam pipe, and a hinged crossbar as evidenced by the two parallel rows of three rivets halfway up the front of the wrapper. The trailing bogie axle had been replaced with a solid one and round-head rivets had been used on the leading and driving wheel balance weights. The trailing wheel weight, however, was still flush riveted. Steam sanding was fitted, the crosshead vacuum pump had been removed, the engine had no makers' plate, and the cruciform rib type had replaced the original axlebox covers on the riveted Mk 1 tender.

G. W. SHARPE

shaded vermilion and glazed lake, or countershaded, numbers and letters.

In the years that followed, the LMS introduced variations in the style of letters and numbers used. The first came in 1936 and although short-lived, was applied to many of the Class 5s that will be the subject of the next *Profile* on the class as well as a few of the first series that were repainted at the time. As far as we are aware, none of the locomotives that were renumbered received replacement smokebox door number plates cast in this style.

During the war, repainted engines were unlined with a variety of lettering and numbering styles and a few locomotives were then turned out in the LMS 1946-style livery. In early BR days there were many different number and lettering styles applied to the engines but eventually all received the standard mixed traffic lining and Gill Sans characters. There were, however, several different sizes and positions of numbers as well as variations in such things as smokebox number plates. Tender sides had 'BRITISH RAILWAYS' lettering for a

while on some examples but eventually the lion-on-wheel emblem was used. This was later replaced by the lion-holding-wheel crest and in the 1960s overhead warning flashes appeared. Four engines in the 5000–5224 series were named after Scottish regiments – the only Class 5s to be named in either LMS or BR service. The foregoing is only a very brief resume of Class 5 liveries, full details being given in *LMS Locomotive Profile No. 5*.

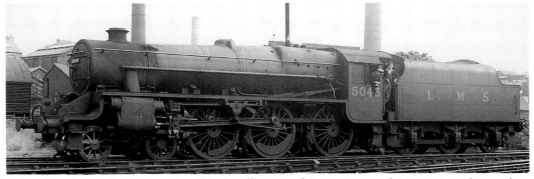

*During the Second World War, lining was omitted when engines were repainted. Some locomotives were merely retouched rather than being fully repainted and often had the numbers and letters hand painted in plain pale yellow over the existing transfers. In the later war years, some had the cabside numerals moved up to just underneath the windows with the power classification below them. The next three pictures show locomotives in wartime unlined black with different sizes and styles of numbers in the high position. This view illustrates what may be termed a common wartime repaint with No. 5043 having 12in unshaded numerals. As recorded in LMS Locomotive Profiles No. 5, earlier in the war this engine had the same size shaded vermilion numerals, so it is possible that as seen here they had been painted over in pale yellow. In 1947 it was one of relatively few engines we know of that was repainted plain black with 1946-style transfers. Although holes had been cut in the boiler clothing for extra washout plugs at the top of the front ring, they were blanked off when this photograph was taken. Long liner plates had been fitted in the smokebox, the boiler was a 21-element, domeless example and the cylinder clothing had both rectangular and large circular access covers. Bogie axles had been replaced with solid ones, crosshead vacuum pump and hot-water de-sanding removed, and steam sanding fitted in lieu of gravity sanding. Ribbed axlebox covers had replaced plain ones on the riveted Mk 1 tender.* AUTHORS' COLLECTION

*The transitional period between nationalisation and the advent of standard, lined BR livery brought an almost endless variety of livery styles.* LMS Locomotive Profiles No. 5 *gives many more details but we have selected four pictures (three overleaf) to illustrate some of them. Another locomotive that went from 12in numbers to 10in ones in the mid-1940s was 5029 seen here. In this case, however, the engine appears to have been completely repainted rather than just patch-painted and both numbers and letters were yellow, shaded vermilion, transfers with the former spaced further apart than usual. The power classification, also freshly applied, was very close to the number. The steam pipe clothing had the longer recess with which the first ten Vulcan Foundry engines were built but the original, hollow bogie axles had been replaced by solid ones. Cylinder clothing and sanding arrangement were as previously described for engines at this time, rain gutters had been added, and although the buffer beam had been drilled for snow plough attachment, there were no brackets below it. The engine was coupled to a Mk 2 welded tender. Note the large clinker shovel leaning against the cab side. These were kept at sheds and used when the fire was being cleaned or dropped and were not carried on the locomotive.* R. K. BLENCOWE

At the beginning of the British Railways era, some engines were plain black and wore the shortlived 'M' prefix to their LMS numbers in a variety of styles. Further details are given in LMS Locomotive Profiles No. 5. Here we see No. 5077 from 24E, Blackpool, with its number in what appears to have been 12in characters similar to the 1946 LMS style but slightly thinner. They were set in line with the tender lettering with a 6in 'M' below and the power classification above. Its Mk 1 riveted tender had 'BRITISH RAILWAYS' in 8in Gill Sans lettering. The smokebox had front liner plates with rivets on the door ring and the domeless, 21-element boiler had extra forward washout plugs. The combination lever was one of the straight, fluted variety fitted to later Vulcan Foundry engines such as this, and details of sanding, balance weights, etc. were normal for a locomotive at this time.

*A variation of the 'M' prefix plain black livery can be seen in this photograph of 5018. Ten-inch, 1946-pattern numerals without maroon edging or inset lining were set just below the cab windows with the 'M' added ahead of them and the power classification figure '5' almost in line with the platform below the '0'. The engine was built at Crewe in May 1935 and when the photograph was taken had a 21-element, domeless boiler with an unusual top feed cover that had no separate clack fairings. The smokebox had extra liner plate rivets at the side but not the front and the balance weights were normal for the time but the tender was a welded Mk 2. AUTHORS' COLLECTION*

*In this view we can see Crewe-built 45013 in plain black with its number applied using 10in characters, similar to the LMS 1946 type without edging or lining, that are widely spaced and set in line with the platform. The power classification '5' was immediately under the cab windows and the tender still carried 14in yellow, shaded vermilion, LMS letters. At this time the engine had no smokebox number plate but later received one with 1946-style numerals. The tube cleaner cock was mounted higher on the smokebox than it had been originally. Other details of the boiler, smokebox, cylinder clothing, etc. can be ascertained from descriptions given previously but it is notable that two of the three tender axlebox covers visible were the plain type originally fitted to the first fifty Vulcan Foundry examples.*

*R. K. BLENCOWE*

A relatively common combination in early BR days was that displayed by plain black No. 45113. The smokebox door carried a 7C, Holyhead, plate and the number plate had scroll-and-serif numerals, the power class was immediately below the cab windows and the cabside numerals were unlined 1946-style set halfway between window and platform level and closer together than on 45136. Some engines painted in this style were coupled to tenders carrying 'BRITISH RAILWAYS' whilst others had plain tenders, but the one paired with 45113 still wore 'LMS' lettering that is just visible under the grime. AUTHORS' COLLECTION

Some engines had their new BR number hand painted in styles peculiar to the painter. One such was Armstrong Whitworth 45136, seen at Perth in June 1949. Apart from the number and the red buffer beam, there was no other decoration to relieve the plain black paint scheme. The top feed delivery pipes were set in between the proud position seen on the first Vulcan Foundry engines and that of most others below the level of the boiler clothing. The top feed cover was the type normally used with domed boilers. Note the automatic tablet exchanger on the cab side. These were put onto and taken off engines as required for operating over single-line sections equipped for them.

The official typeface selected by BR for numbering and lettering was Gill Sans. Vulcan Foundry No. 45052, stationed when photographed at Aston, as shown by its 3D shedcode plate, is seen still displaying scroll-and-serif numbers on its smokebox door plate but wearing the new style of 8in numerals on the cab side. Engine and tender were unlined and there was no power class figure on the cab or lettering of any sort on the tender. The boiler was a 24-element, domed example rebuilt from a 14-element, domeless type, the smokebox had liner plates at the front but not the side, and the bogie axles were solid replacements. The tube cleaner cock was mounted higher up the smokebox than originally and there were no makers' plates. Leading coupled wheels had round-head rivets on the balance weights but the others were still flush-riveted.

E. KEARNS

The livery style settled on for Class 5s after the middle of 1948 was based on the old L&NWR lined black. Details of the lining can be found in LMS Locomotive Profiles No. 5, as can descriptions of some of the variations in lettering, numbers and symbols used. This photograph shows an early variation of the scheme as applied to No. 45111, then stationed at 7C Holyhead, at Crewe North in December 1948 with Gill Sans smokebox door numbers and 8in cream Gill Sans numerals on the cab side in line with 10in Gill Sans tender lettering. The power classification '5' was close below the number. The engine's frames had obviously been changed as they had Armstrong Whitworth plates on them whereas the smokebox wore the Vulcan Foundry plates with which it had been built. Other details of the locomotive can be determined from previous descriptions. The tender was a Mk 2 welded version.

AUTHORS' COLLECTION

*Apart from one detail, 45103 was turned out from Crewe in 1949 wearing what by then was the standard livery for a Class 5. Paint-work was black with cream, red and grey lining, all characters were Gill Sans with 8in numerals on the cab side between window and platform level, power class '5' was displayed above the number, and the tender had the 'monocyling lion' BR emblem on its sides. The one difference from the norm was that the figure '4' was much smaller than the other numbers.*
R. S. CARPENTER

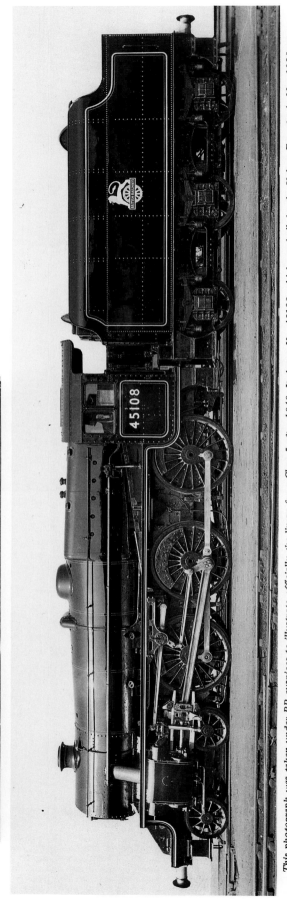

*This photograph was taken under BR auspices to illustrate officially the livery for a Class 5 after 1948. It shows No. 45108, which was built by the Vulcan Foundry in May 1935, as repainted following renumbering in January 1949. Included in the paint scheme was red lining on the cylinder clothing bands, which was not applied to all engines turned out in this livery. Cabside numbers were 8in Gill Sans, whereas for some time St. Rollox used 10in ones, and the first style of BR emblem was applied to the tender sides. The sloping-throatplate boiler with which the engine was fitted in June 1948 had its top feed on the second ring and the crosshead still had the rear attachment where the drive to the vacuum pump had been. Whilst leading and intermediate coupled wheel balance weights had been repaired using round-head rivets, those on the trailing wheels were still flush. The engine was coupled to a riveted Mk 1 tender, which type it retained all its life.*
BRITISH RAILWAYS

*Typical of an engine painted at St. Rollox from late 1948 to the mid-1950s was 45168, seen here at Corkerhill in September 1952. Cabside numerals were 10in Gill Sans and there does not appear to have been any lining on the cylinder clothing bands, although it is difficult to be certain from this picture. Locomotives based in Scotland exchanged tenders more often than did those south of the border and between April 1950 and being photographed here, 45168 was paired with welded, part-welded and riveted varieties. Note the round-head rivets on the driving wheel balance weight, steam sanding and train staff holder on the cab side.*
AUTHORS' COLLECTION

By the early 1960s, many Class 5s were in a fairly decrepit and filthy state. An engine on standby to work the Royal train, however, would always be in good condition, clean and thoroughly examined before the fire was raised. In the early 1960s No. 45003 was photographed at Stafford with steam up waiting to replace the English Electric Type 4 diesel, were it to fail, that was rostered to haul the Royal train. Built at Crewe in March 1935, the engine had been fitted with a 21-element, domeless boiler, solid bogie axles and AWS by the time this picture was taken. It still had support brackets to the fronts of its cylinder drain pipes, hollow coupled axles and flush-riveted balance weights. The smokebox had extra liner plates and a hinged crossbar, as shown by the extra rivets, and it can just be made out that there were access covers for washout plugs in the boiler clothing ahead of the top feed. The engine was coupled to a Mk 2 welded tender No. 10941 with late BR-style spring hangers and radially ribbed axlebox covers that are the only examples of this type known to us. Livery was fully lined with post-1956 heraldic crests and overhead warning flashes.

J. B. BUCKNALL

*No. 45219 was one of the last few engines built with a vertical-throatplate boiler. Delivered by Armstrong Whitworth in November 1935, it was photographed at Low Moor in about 1960 after over-head warning flashes had been applied to the frames, boiler behind the top feed, firebox sides and tender front. Although partly obscured by steam, it can be determined that the cylinder drain pipes no longer had a support bracket at their front ends and the tube cleaner cock was connected to a union high on the smokebox by an external pipe. The locomotive had been fitted with AWS and was coupled to a part-welded Mk 1 tender that it had received in May 1948.*
AUTHORS' COLLECTION

*This picture was taken at St. Rollox Works sometime after 45175 was fitted with AWS in September 1960 and shows what we suppose to have been an engine that had just undergone repair and was waiting for a visit to the paint shop. The smokebox had obviously been patched at the front and many of the rivets were new around the rear of the wrapper and the cab footsteps. The locomotive number had been chalked onto the wheel centres, suggesting that they had been removed, and applied crudely to the cab side in what appears to have been whitewash. It can just be discerned that the gangway doors had rubber extensions. Note that all the coupled axles were still hollow.*  AUTHORS' COLLECTION

Towards the ends of their lives, some Class 5s became so filthy and decrepit that simply identifying individual engines could be difficult. This is a photograph of 45038 taken in January 1965, identification being possible from the relatively clean smokebox door plate. Whether there was any lining under the grime is impossible to state but the cabside numbers, whilst illegible, are just visible and the BR crest on the tender can be made out through close examination. The most obvious emblems are the overhead warning flashes on the frames, firebox and boiler barrel. As well as the presence of warning flashes, the smokebox door lamp holder had been moved to a lower position on the left-hand side so that enginemen changing lamps would not be placed close to the wires. The engine was equipped with AWS, as shown by the electrical conduit along the platform angle and the small timing reservoir in front of the cab. No. 45038 was built by the Vulcan Foundry in September 1934 and was withdrawn from service in February 1968. AUTHORS' COLLECTION

This photograph of No. 45042 at Bristol Barrow Road in November 1965 was taken from a relatively unusual viewpoint. Among the details revealed are the access plates on the boiler clothing for washout plugs in front of the top feed and the ventilation holes in the cab front. The locomotive was in a fairly run-down condition with no covers over the firebox shoulder washout plugs and a poorly fitting clothing panel between top feed and firebox. It was fitted with AWS, the small cylinder in front of the cab being the timing reservoir, and had its top lamp holder moved down to the left-hand side of the smokebox door because of overhead electrification. Although filthy, both engine and tender were lined and the home shed, 'MOLD JUNCTION', was painted on the front buffer beam, indicating that its last repaint had been at St. Rollox.      A. G. ELLIS

*Through freight trains from Perth to Inverness were regular Class 5 turns. In this picture, 5160 is seen about to leave Perth Highland yard in charge of the 2.35 p.m. with three LMS and one LNER meat vans immediately behind the tender. Since being built by Armstrong Whitworth in July 1935, the only apparent alteration to the engine had been the removal of its crosshead vacuum pump and the addition of the tablet exchanger. Note the polished metal items on the smokebox.*

AUTHORS' COLLECTION

# LOCOMOTIVES IN SERVICE

*Express passenger trains were not always lengthy — a point illustrated admirably by this picture of No. 5069 at Millers Dale in June 1936. The five-coach formation consisted of four passenger-carrying vehicles, the leading one being an ex-Midland Railway six-wheel passenger brake van. The others appear to have been an ex-Midland Railway clerestory composite followed by three LMS standard vehicles — two third brakes flanking a composite. The locomotive, built at the Vulcan Foundry in 1934, appears to have been in original condition and the 19C shedplate indicates that it was stationed at Canklow.*                                                    AUTHORS' COLLECTION

The LMS Stanier Class 5 4–6–0s were remarkable locomotives and one measure of their popularity with railwaymen was the assertion that, 'They were the engines that won the war.' It would be difficult to find an engineman who did not like them while many preferred them above all other classes. They were not perfect, but for their time they were extremely good engines. In this section we are going to examine some of the wide-ranging duties they carried out during their lifetime in both joint-stock company and national ownership.

When the class was being schemed, one of the criteria was that they should be able to run over at least 70% of the LMS system. As far as we can see, the Class 5s route availability was rather greater. The lines over which classes of locomotives were allowed to run were determined by the company's Chief Civil Engineer and was based upon a number of factors, expressed simply as would they foul any fixed structures, were they too heavy for any bridges and, at a more local level, could they run through certain sidings or sharp curves? For example, there were some lines where a class was permitted to run, but only at reduced speeds.

In *LMS Locomotive Profile No. 5* we discussed the introduction into service of Nos. 5000–5224 and further details of their employment after 1935 will be included in future *Profiles* dealing with the remaining Class 5s. In order to complement those publications, however, we will continue the 'Engines in Service' theme in this book and try to illustrate some of the types of trains that they worked as well as some of the districts in which they ran.

Examination of a number of editions of *Routes Over Which Engines May Run*, confirms that the class could operate over more than 90% of the old LMS system. Furthermore, during the post-1948 period they were also used on other regions of British Railways without too many restrictions. We give a few examples below but the list is far from comprehensive.

On the old Midland Division of the LMS they were restricted from running over many of the colliery lines in the North and East Midlands and South Yorkshire. There were also some branch lines where they were not permitted to run – for instance those to Ilkeston Town, Nailsworth, Thornbury, and Wirksworth. An example of severe bridge restrictions was to be found on the old SMJ section between the junctions at Broom and Ravenstone Wood

Junction. There, the bridges at Towcester and over the Euston–Rugby line could only be crossed by Class 5s at less than 15 mph and providing that there was no engine on the adjoining line at the time. Another line that was subject to speed limits was the thirty-three mile branch between Ashchurch and Barnt Green where an overall speed limit of 25 mph applied; this, however, was later removed.

Similar restrictions applied on the other operating divisions of the LMS and indeed elsewhere, two examples being the lines between Clapham Junction and East Croydon via Crystal Palace and between East Croydon and Three Bridges. Notwithstanding these minor restrictions, the popular view that the Class 5 could go anywhere was generally true and they could be found from the far north of

The Class 5s were routinely employed on express passenger trains, such as on this occasion when 5096 was pictured at Beauchief near Sheffield. A number of such trains conveyed coaches from other companies that could be attached or detached during the course of a journey or even run right through. An example of this was when GWR coaches from the West Country were attached at Bristol to LMS trains for destinations in the north of England. The first two vehicles behind 5096 were such coaches, the train probably being a Bristol–Leeds and Bradford service. Engine and tender were as built with 21-element, domeless boiler, Vulcan Foundry plates on the smokebox, and closely-spaced letters.            A. G. ELLIS

The first twenty-five Vulcan Foundry engines were built without a step between the frames in front of the smokebox, and feed pipes to the top feed clacks on the first fifty were mounted outside the boiler clothing, as seen in this view of 5044 in the summer of 1936. The taller chimney fitted to the first fifty Vulcan Foundry locomotives is also evident, as is the lack of rain gutters at the edges of the cab roof. Other characteristics of all contractor-built engines included the round-head bolts at each end of the buffer beam where it was attached to the platform angles, lack of front steam-heating hoses, and smokebox-mounted makers' plates. Note the lack of firebox shoulder washout inspection doors, characteristic of boilers originally built with fourteen superheater flues and the first three 21-element units, and the plain section, cranked combination lever used on Nos. 5000-5069. The narrow spacing of the tender lettering was typical of contractor-built engines, whilst characteristic of the first fifty Vulcan Foundry examples were the plain axlebox covers. The locomotive was carrying express passenger train headcode and was probably a Bristol (where it was photographed) to Bradford service.

AUTHORS' COLLECTION

Scotland to stations in towns alongside the English Channel. In this section we have included some pictures that we believe illustrate this rather well.

From an operating standpoint, the route availability of any particular class was but one question. Another important consideration was what weight of train could they haul over various sections of line? We will try to put their haulage capacity into focus by comparing it with other well-known LMS classes of locomotives.

With a few exceptions and subject to the ruling gradients, the full load for a passenger train hauled by a Class 5, i.e., the maximum tare weight of the train without passengers and luggage, was 370 tons where the gradients were steep or 435

*The LMS headlamp code of one lamp over the left-hand buffer and one on the smokebox door denoted an express freight or cattle train with the continuous brake operative on not less than four vehicles that were connected to the engine. These trains were indicated in the working timetable by a Maltese Cross and consequently were commonly referred to by railwaymen as 'Maltese' the signal box bell code for them being '2-pause-2-pause-3'. The same headlamp code could also indicate an express freight with a limited load of vehicles not fitted with continuous brakes, the reduced braking power available to the driver meaning that it would run at lower speed. The bell code in this case was '3-pause-2'. This undated picture shows No. 5179 with a 'Maltese' consisting of goods vans and open goods wagons that were sheeted over to protect the contents from inclement weather. The first four vans were equipped with automatic vacuum brakes and constituted what was known as the 'fitted head'. The locomotive was built by Armstrong Whitworth in September 1935 and appears to have been in original condition.* AUTHORS' COLLECTION

*Although No. 5029 was carrying the same headlamp code as 5179 in the previous photograph when it was photographed at Blair Athol in 1935, the composition of its train was rather different. The four leading vehicles appear to have been ex-Highland Railway twin bolster trucks carrying rails and fitted with grease axleboxes, which would prohibit the train from running at the normal booked speed of a 'Maltese'. The remainder of the train was made up of cattle wagons that were probably empty. No. 5029 was built by the Vulcan Foundry in September 1934 and had yet to be fitted with a step between the frames below its smokebox. It had all the other characteristics of the earliest Vulcan Foundry engines with hollow bogie axles, tall chimney, long steam pipe recesses, smokebox-mounted makers' plates, domeless boiler without firebox shoulder washout doors, external water delivery pipes and no rain gutters. The lettering on its Mk 1 riveted tender was spaced at 40in.* AUTHORS' COLLECTION

*This delightful period piece shows Vulcan Foundry-built 5036 running into Millers Dale from the north in July 1938 with an ordinary passenger train watched by two enthralled children. The train is an interesting formation of a full brake and five other vehicles, two of which appear to be 3rd brakes. The locomotive still had its tall chimney and makers' plates on the smokebox but had acquired a 21-element boiler with washout doors on the firebox shoulders, steam sanding, access covers on the sides and shoulders of the cylinder clothing, and rain gutters on the cab roof. The Mk 1 riveted tender retained plain axlebox covers. Livery was the 1936 block style.*    E. R. MORTON

*Many of the first locomotives delivered were sent to work on the Northern Division and the class was well known in Scotland throughout its service. No. 5014 was built at Crewe in April 1935 and is seen in this 11th August 1939 photograph hauling an empty coaching stock train at Inverness, the leading vehicle being a sleeping car. The locomotive was built with a domeless, 21-element boiler, as shown by the firebox shoulder washout doors, but wearing 10in cabside numerals. The tender was of welded construction.* COLLECTION P. TATLOW

*Although cross-country, single-track lines were probably not considered by many as the natural setting where the new Class 5s would be found, they were used on several such routes almost from the beginning of their service. No. 5008 of Inverness shed was photographed in August 1939 at Invershin on the old Highland line north of Inverness working a passenger train composed of at least four passenger-carrying coaches, the leading vehicle being some form of slatted van that was probably being used for milk traffic. As it was summer time, it is not surprising that the front steam-heating equipment had been removed for storage and, possibly, overhaul. At the other end of the weather scale, the buffer beam had been drilled for the fitting of a snow plough. Although it was built at Crewe, the locomotive had round-head rivets at the ends of its buffer beam and both round and rectangular access covers had been fitted to its cylinder clothing by the time this photograph was taken.* L. HANSON

The headlamp code of one in the centre and one above on No. 5010 shows it to have been working a through freight train when it was photographed in Scotland sometime between 1946, when extra washout plugs were fitted in the first barrel ring, and January 1949 when it was renumbered 45010. The train was quite light and appears to have been made up of about twelve covered goods vans and seven open goods wagons. The description of such a train in the 1937 appendix to the working timetable was 'Through freight train or ballast train conveying workmen and running not less than fifteen miles without stopping'. In June 1950, when British Railways rationalised most of the previously separate company headcodes, this became Class H. Alterations to the locomotive since it was built by Crewe Works in March 1935 included round-head rivets on the ends of the buffer beam, the addition of both circular and rectangular access plates in the cylinder clothing, removal of the vacuum pump and hot-water de-sanding apparatus, and fitting of steam in lieu of gravity sanding. The boiler was a 21-element, domeless example and the smokebox had received extra liner plates at the sides as well as a door support bracket. Note the automatic tablet exchanger fitted to the cab side.                    GAVIN WILSON

We are not sure where this picture was taken but suspect that the date was about 1947. No. 5009 was hauling a through freight train, as shown by the lamp on the smokebox door and another just visible behind the vacuum hose in the centre of the buffer beam. At the time, the engine was stationed at Carlisle Kingmoor and was equipped to receive a snow plough with drilled buffer beam and fixing brackets. Its boiler was a 21-element, domeless example and the smokebox was without extra liner plates, still with a fixed crossbar, and displaying a support bracket for the door. The number was applied to the cab side in what seem on close examination to have been hand-painted characters and the tender was a Mk 2 welded version that the engine acquired in March 1942. AUTHORS' COLLECTION

tons on sections where they were less severe. When running with a limited load, which allowed the train to be timed to run at a higher speed between stations where it was booked to stop, the weight was generally either 320 or 380 tons. The loading for the more powerful 5XP 'Jubilee' or 'Patriot' Classes was 415 or 495 tons full load and 365 or 430 tons limited load, whereas for a Class 4P Standard Compound 4–4–0 it was 320 or 380 tons full load and 280 or 330 tons limited load. The average tare weight of an LMS standard corridor coach at this time was about 30 tons, so it is possible to gain a rough

idea of how many carriages the various classes could pull.

The Class 5s excelled on express freight trains and their standard loading for a Fully Fitted No. 1 train, which had to be hauled by a passenger engine, was 45 wagons. This compared with 39 wagons when hauled by a Compound or 50 wagons with a Class 5XP. We should point out that the standard load was reduced if the train was to run unassisted over sections of line that included steep gradients. The No. 2 Fitted freight train was not timed to run as quickly as a No. 1 Fitted but consisted of more wagons and could be hauled by a freight

engine. The standard load for a Class 5 on such a train was 50 wagons, which also applied to a Horwich mogul, whereas for a Compound or Class 4F 0–6–0 it was 43 and a 5XP could take 55.

Finally, it is worth comparing the haulage powers when engines were working mineral trains. A good example is the line between Birmingham and Derby that did not have any gradients worthy of note and over which a Class 5 was allowed to haul 62 loaded 13-ton mineral wagons, a Class 4F 0–6–0 could take 56, a Class 8F 2–8–0 was allowed 82, and a Garratt could pull a hundred.

*Until June 1950, the London, Midland Region of British Railways continued to use the LMS headlamp and bell codes for train description. The lamp code seen in this September 1948 view of one lamp over the right-hand buffer and one in the centre, which was signalled under the bell code of '1-pause-1-pause-3', indicated a parcels, newspaper, fish, meat, fruit, milk, horse, or perishable train composed of coaching stock. Whilst this description obviously applied to the three leading carriages of the train, which were passenger brake vans, it does not appear at first glance to have been entirely correct for the two covered vans at the rear. The explanation is that certain goods vehicles with 10ft wheelbases and having the correct axleboxes, springs and buffers, could be attached to such trains, which would seem to apply in this case. No. 5033 was approaching Watford tunnel with an up train from Rugby when this picture was taken and was fitted with a 24-element, vertical-throatplate boiler – a type that it first acquired in May 1942. It appears to have been painted in unlined black with scroll-and-serif characters. It is impossible to state whether the letters and cabside numbers were shaded. Less than two months after this photograph was taken the engine was renumbered 45033.*
E. D. BRUTON

*No. 5075 working an ordinary passenger train between Manchester and Wigan. The three coaches were probably a 3rd brake, composite, another 3rd brake and an all-third class coach. The shed code plates show that 5075 was from 25C, Goole. It was not unusual for engines to be diagrammed for two or three days work away from their home depots and sometimes this work included trains that were of a minor nature. 5075 appears to have been painted in wartime plain black livery, with yellow, shaded vermilion scroll-and-serif transfers on cab and tender.*
AUTHORS' COLLECTION

*The headlamp code carried by breakdown trains varied. If the train was proceeding to clear the line, it ran under the Class A headcode of one lamp over each buffer and was given priority over all other traffic. Otherwise, it would carry the same headlamp code as an ordinary passenger train, namely one headlamp on the smokebox, and attract the appropriate priority. This undated, early British Railways period photograph shows No. 45011 with the Haymarket breakdown train. In addition to the crane and the loose equipment that was required, breakdown trains included vehicles with messing facilities for the men, who were usually fitters from the shed where it was stationed. If called out in an emergency, the train would be hauled by the first available locomotive. No. 45011 was fitted with a 28-element, sloping-throatplate, domed boiler of the later type having its top feed on the first ring. The latter was of post-1947 pattern with the clacks incorporated into a centre casting and having a shroud over the setscrews. In order to carry such a boiler, any of the first 225 Class 5s needed its frames modifying or, as in this case, to receive already altered ones. Whilst the engine had been built at Crewe, the frames seen here carried Armstrong Whitworth makers' plates. The front steam heating apparatus had been removed and round-head rivets had been used when repairing balance weights.*

AUTHORS' COLLECTION

This photograph of No. 45081 piloting another, unidentified, Class 5 on a parcels train was taken in late 1948 or 1949. The locomotive was painted plain black and did not have a smokebox door numberplate. Its BR number had been applied to the cab side in LMS 1946-style numerals without inset maroon lining, set with their lower edges in line with the platform and having power classification '5' below. The Mk 1 riveted tender carried 'BRITISH RAILWAYS' in 8in Gill Sans letters. It can just be seen that the buffer beam had been drilled for the fitting of a snow plough and is apparent that the smokebox had side and front liner plates but retained a fixed cross-bar.                              AUTHORS' COLLECTION

No. 5218, photographed with an ordinary passenger train at Sanderson's Sidings, Worsley in March 1948. The three coaches were probably a 3rd brake, composite, and another 3rd brake. The shed code plate shows 5218 to have been stationed at 25B, Huddersfield. It is seen here in wartime plain black livery.
                              AUTHORS' COLLECTION

*This picture of 45199, taken in June 1951 at Brock water troughs between Preston and Lancaster, shows that at this time a variety of coaching stock was pressed into use for summer service special trains. Among an assortment of vehicles, the first and third carriages were ex-L&YR. The engine was fitted with a 24-element, vertical-throatplate, domed boiler rebuilt from one of the first fifty-seven Type 3Bs that originally had a 14-element superheater and no dome. Clothing on its firebox and second ring of the barrel were heavily streaked with lime.*

AUTHORS' COLLECTION

Whereas it was relatively unusual to see two Class 5s in charge of a freight train, the addition of a pilot engine to a passenger train could be seen on a regular basis. This picture of No. 45053 piloting another, unidentified, Class 5 was taken in May 1952 and shows the 5.30 p.m. express passenger train from Aberdeen, complete with 'The Granite City' headboard, approaching Perth on what was clearly a fine spring evening. No. 45053 was carrying a 24-element vertical-throatplate, domed boiler without firebox shoulder washout doors but with blanking plates in its firebox clothing. The top feed cover was round rather than the transverse type intended for use with such boilers, a feature most often seen on engines repaired at St. Rollox. The train engine was fitted with a 28-element, sloping throatplate boiler with a post-1947 type of top feed having a transverse cover and raised fairing over the setscrews. No. 45053's tender was a welded Mk 2 whereas the train engine was coupled to a part-welded Mk 1. Other details that had been changed over the years since 45053 was built can be determined from the information given elsewhere. Note that the cabside numerals were mounted at differing levels on the two locomotives. AUTHORS' COLLECTION

Even though the Class 5s were powerful engines, they still needed piloting if the load was more than the tonnage they were allowed to take over a given section of line. In this picture No. 45126 is seen piloting 44900, one of the later members of the class that will be the subject of another work in this series, over the Leeds–Settle–Carlisle line on an 8.30 a.m. St. Pancras–Edinburgh express passenger train. The picture was taken during the afternoon of 3rd June 1952 as the train was crossing Smardale viaduct and shortly about to enter Crosby Garrett tunnel. No. 45126 was carrying the same type of boiler with which it was built, i.e. a 21-element, vertical-throatplate, domeless type with firebox shoulder washout doors, with extra washout plugs fitted on top of the first ring. The top feed cover is the type normally fitted to domed boiler locomotives; this arrangement was a particular feature of St. Rollox works. The tender was a Mk 1 riveted example, which was replaced by a part-welded one three months after this photograph was taken. Stationed at Carlisle Kingmoor, 45126 had been repainted at St. Rollox and, typically for the time, carried 10in Gill Sans cabside numbers set with their lower edges in line with the platform angle. Although difficult to see in the deep shadow, a close examination reveals that the shed name was painted on 45126's buffer beam, which was another St. Rollox feature. The buffer beam was drilled for the fitting of a snow plough and mounting brackets were attached to the frames. Both engines had train staff holders on their cab sides for working over single-line sections.
E. D. BRUTON

After nationalisation, ex-LMS locomotives found their way onto routes where previously they were unknown. An example of this was the ex-NBR/LNER West Highland line from Glasgow to Mallaig via Fort William over which the engines ran with conspicuous success. In this May 1954 study, 45084 is seen in Glen Ogle heading what the headlamp code indicates was a Class K train as described elsewhere and consisting, as far as can be seen, of a 16-ton mineral wagon plus assorted vans and empty cattle wagons. The engine was carrying a sloping-throatplate, domed boiler with the top feed on the second ring that it received in August 1950 and which was replaced by a domeless type six months after the picture was taken. The top feed cover was one of the rounded ones normally only seen on domeless boilers. Even though it was working over a single-line section, the engine was not fitted with an automatic tablet exchanger as the WHR did not have the necessary trackside equipment.

AUTHORS' COLLECTION

*This rather atmospheric picture of Motherwell-stationed No. 45152 with a Class F unfitted express freight train was taken near Abington between Carstairs and Beattock on the old Caledonian main line in July 1956. Although Class F trains by definition had limited brake power, it was a requirement that all vehicles had oil rather than grease-filled axleboxes. The boiler fitted to No. 45152 was one of the first three 21-element, domeless examples that were originally made for Nos. 5007-5009, as shown by the fact that it had no firebox shoulder washout doors. After October 1940, these were the only domeless boilers without the doors. Note, however, that the firebox clothing had cover plates where there had been doors on a previous boiler.* AUTHORS' COLLECTION

*Although at first sight No. 45122 appears to have been in charge of a Class F express goods train when it was photographed at Appleby in July 1954, the picture is deceptive. The locomotive was actually shunting and when photographed was making up its train in the siding behind the rearmost tank wagon. Apart from the low-sided wagon behind the tender, which was probably being used as a 'runner', the train was made up of milk tanks and it is quite possible that when it was ready to depart the classification would have become C or D. The locomotive's buffer beam had been drilled to take a snow plough and support brackets were fitted to its frames. The smokebox was possibly a replacement without any evidence of extra liner plates but with a high-mounted tube cleaner cock and door support bracket. The number plate had been cast at St. Rollox with characteristic typeface to the numerals and there are indications that the door was burned either side of the shed code plate through air leaking between it and the front ring. The locomotive was coupled to a Mk 2 welded tender, which type it ran with between January 1947 and December 1949, June 1950 and April 1957, and from May 1958 until withdrawal.* AUTHORS' COLLECTION

Kyle of Lochalsh provides a beautiful setting for this picture of No. 45132 being piloted by No. 44783, which was one of the later Class 5s built at Horwich in 1947, while working a goods train in August 1957. The 10in numerals on the cab side of No. 45132 were characteristic of an engine painted at St. Rollox, and both locomotives were fitted with automatic tablet exchangers.

J. A. G. H. COLTAS

In some parts of the country, passenger trains were quite light, as this photograph of 45179 with just three coaches at Nairn, between Inverness and Elgin, on 3rd August 1954 shows. The train was the 12.15 p.m. Perth–Inverness and consisted of a composite, 3rd brake and passenger brake van. The engine's buffer beam was drilled for the fitting of a snow plough and mounting brackets were attached to the frames and the locomotive is fitted with a top feed cover normally used with domed boilers.
AUTHORS' COLLECTION

Several sections of single line on the LMS saw express passenger trains on a regular basis, one of them being the 'Port Road' to Stranraer on the Portpatrick & Wigtownshire Joint line. This picture, taken on 11th July 1955 near Stranraer, shows 45126 in charge of the 12.17 p.m. Stranraer Harbour to Carlisle – a train that largely carried passengers who had travelled by ferry from Northern Ireland. The locomotive's buffer beam had been repaired using snap-head rivets.
J. E. EDGINGTON

This photograph shows a down Class F train with Crewe North No. 45150 in charge leaving Preston on 24th March 1957. Class F was defined as 'Express freight, livestock, perishable or ballast train not fitted with continuous brakes' and indicated that the only braking power available to the driver was that on the locomotive and tender. The leading wagon was a wooden-bodied 13T mineral wagon with bottom door followed by an ex-Southern Railway covered goods van. As far as can be seen, the remainder of the train was made up of open goods wagons containing rather bulky loads covered by tarpaulin sheets.
AUTHORS' COLLECTION

This photograph shows 45004 at Barrow Road, Bristol in 1961 still carrying a vertical-throatplate, domeless boiler, albeit one of the later, 21-element examples first made for the second batch of Vulcan Foundry and Armstrong Whitworth locomotives – note the shoulder washout doors on the firebox. Its frames had also been changed and a close inspection shows that they carried Armstrong Whitworth plates above the front platform. The engine was coupled to a welded Mk 2 tender, which type it acquired in February 1945 and retained until withdrawal in September 1966, and had been fitted with AWS in January 1959. The plate below the buffer beam was to protect the AWS receiver mounted on a stretcher between the bogie frames from damage by the front coupling and the cylinder on the platform in front of the cab was a vacuum reservoir. Since being built, the engine had acquired extra liner plates at the bottom and front of the smokebox, as shown by the extra rivets on the wrapper and door ring, the retaining bracket had been removed from the cylinder drain pipes, and access holes with covers had been provided in the cylinder clothing. The circular cover, which gave access to the steam chest drain and oil pipe adaptor for the top barrel feed, was the larger type that in the 1940s replaced the small version fitted after 1935. Round-head rivets had replaced the original flush ones at either end of the buffer beam, the driving axle was solid, and round-head rivets had been used to repair the gravity sanding with which the engine was built and the hot-water de-sanding apparatus had been removed. Although overhead electrification warning flashes had been applied to the front frames and firebox shoulders, the lamp holder on the smokebox door was still at the top.

AUTHORS' COLLECTION

This photograph, taken at Crewe South in April 1966, shows 45004 five months before withdrawal. By that time, it had been fitted with one of the first fifty-seven type 3B boilers that had been rebuilt with a 24-element superheater and dome-mounted regulator. These boilers are immediately recognisable as they were the only ones with domes but without firebox shoulder washout doors. A close examination of the print, however, reveals that the firebox clothing had blanking plates over the holes where washout doors had been on the engine's previous boiler. This was a common occurrence as the clothing normally remained with a locomotive when boilers were exchanged providing that it was compatible with the new boiler. Apart from the dome and larger superheater, the boiler had also been fitted with extra washout plugs at the top of the first ring immediately behind the smokebox. The tube cleaner cock had been moved further down the smokebox, steam being supplied from a union above the handrail via an external pipe. The driving axle had been changed again and the engine once more had a hollow one. Frames were still of Armstrong Whitworth origin, the makers' plate being visible immediately below the overhead warning flash, and the lamp holder on the smokebox door had been moved to the lower position on the left-hand side for clearance from overhead wires. Livery appears to have been plain black. Both pictures show that steam heating pipes were fitted.

R. K. BLENCOWE

*Although there is a GWR 4—6—0 in the background, this photograph was taken at the ex-Midland Railway Gloucester shed that was finally coded 85C between January 1961 and closure in May 1964. The depot was never modernised and the original coaling stage with inclined approach tracks for the coal wagons remained until it closed. This picture of 45180 was taken on 11th April 1964, which was less than four weeks before all locomotives were transferred to the old GWR depot at Horton Road. The corrugated shed on the far right was the wheel drop and the large building behind was the fitting shop. The general scene was typical of steam sheds during the final years of steam traction and No. 45180's condition, with steam leaking from a number of places and evidence of leaks all over its clothing, was also typical of many steam locomotives at the time.*

AUTHORS' COLLECTION

*No. 45053 was photographed leaving Slateford sidings in January 1962 with a single headlamp over its right-hand buffer indicating a class J mineral or empty wagon train — from the picture we can't tell which it was. The 64C shedplate shows the engine to have been stationed at Dalry Road, Edinburgh. Built at the Vulcan Foundry in November 1934, it was fitted with a 21-element, domeless boiler, long side liner plates and a door support bracket on the smokebox, and AWS. Its original riveted tender had been replaced by a Mk 2 welded version.*         D. P. ROWLAND

*Only four Class 5s ever carried names in LMS or BR service. They were: 5157, named* The Glasgow Highlander *in March 1936; No. 5158, which became* Glasgow Yeomanry *in May 1936; No. 5156, named* Ayrshire Yeomanry, *in September 1936; and 5154, named* Lanarkshire Yeomanry *in April 1937. Various contemporary sources suggest that No. 5155 was named* Queens Edinburgh *from 1942 until 1944, but we have found no confirmatory evidence. The nameplates were attached by countersunk bolts and nuts to backing plates and all appear to have been different shapes and sizes. Crests were displayed on separate plaques, No. 5157's being mounted above the name whereas those of the other three were below. Additionally, No. 5156 had a separate, straight plate with* Earl of Carrick's Own *in very small lettering underneath its plaque and No. 5158 carried* Field Brigade R.A.T.A. *curved underneath and round the foot of the crest. The last surviving named locomotive was No. 45156, which lost its nameplates in the early 1960s and ran for several years with the name painted on the backing plates. By July 1968, these too had been removed but were refitted by the time the engine was withdrawn in August 1968.*
AUTHORS' COLLECTION

# PICTORIAL
## SUPPLEMENT TO
# LMS LOCOMOTIVE PROFILE No. 6
## THE MIXED TRAFFIC CLASS 5s
## PART TWO

by JOHN JENNISON & DAVID CLARKE with DAVID HUNT,
FRED JAMES & BOB ESSERY

*Taken sometime between February 1949 and March 1950, this picture shows Crewe-built 44925 and Horwich 4796 at Slochd Summit on the ex-Highland Railway route to Inverness via Carr Bridge. No. 44925 was heading an ordinary passenger train and had swapped its original part-welded Mk 1 tender for a Mk 2 welded one whilst 4796 had lost its top feed cover, enabling us to see the Ivatt-type top feed as first produced with simple, non-return valve clacks. Neither locomotive seems to have been short of steam after its climb.*

# WALSCHAERTS AND STEPHENSON VALVE GEAR ENGINES
## FROM THE 5225–5499 AND 4658–4999 SERIES

Freshly-painted No. 44845 showed in December 1949 at Crewe North how well the Riddles-inspired L&NWR lined black livery suited Stanier's mixed traffic 4–6–0s. It must have been among the earliest recipients of the BR 'monocycling lion' emblems and was typical of engines painted at Crewe Works from this time. The cylinder clothing bands had red edging, the smokebox door numberplate carried Gill Sans characters, and the 8in cabside numerals had power classification 5s immediately above them. Apart from the livery, the engine and tender appear to have been unaltered since they were built at Crewe in October 1944.

F. A. WYCHERLEY

One of the last three steam locomotives to run in British Railways service was 44871 which, together with 44781, hauled the final steam working from Carlisle to Manchester via the Settle & Carlisle on 11th August 1968. The train was then taken to Liverpool by 45110. No. 44871 was reputedly the last locomotive to remain in steam at a British Railways depot when its fire was dropped at Carnforth on the evening of 13th August. In this photograph, the engine is seen in its final condition with the tube cleaner cock moved to a lower position on the smokebox and fed by an external pipe from a union above the handrail. The cylinder steam pipe casings had originally been fitted to one of the first ten Class 5s to enter service – Vulcan Foundry vertical-throatplate Nos. 5020-5029 – as shown by the large recess visible at the lower end of the right-hand one. The engine was fitted with AWS, as indicated by the vacuum reservoir just in front of the cab, but retained its original type of boiler and tender. It was immaculately presented in fully-lined black livery, including red edging to boiler and cylinder clothing bands, the details of which show up well in this picture. Note that the cream line at the bottom of the front platform angle followed the curve behind the buffer beam whereas the red line carried straight across; on the vast majority of Class 5s all the lining was straight at the front.

AUTHORS' COLLECTION

# FOREWORD

*A trio of mixed traffic Class 5s is seen in this picture taken at an unidentified Scottish shed sometime between February 1953 and March 1958. The one on the left with a 44XXX number and forward top feed boiler is unidentified whilst the middle engine was Derby-built 45497 of April 1944 with its top feed on the second ring. In June 1958, this engine was fitted with a forward top feed boiler, which type it retained until withdrawal. As was common with Scottish Region locomotives, it was fitted with Manson tablet exchanging apparatus on the cab side. The right-hand Class 5 was No. 45389, an Armstrong Whitworth product delivered to the LMS in December 1936 and carrying a forward top feed boiler of the type it had between the dates we have ascribed to the photograph.*
AUTHORS' COLLECTION

This supplement is designed to complement the second volume of *LMS Locomotive Profiles* on the Stanier mixed traffic Class 5s and covers the Walschaerts valve gear engines built after 1935 as well as the solitary Stephenson gear locomotive. It follows on from *Supplement to Profile No. 5* and has been prepared for the same reason, i.e., the large number of high quality photographs that were available to us when *Profile No. 6* was in preparation. Readers of the first supplement will be familiar with the background to this, but for those new to the series, we will reiterate some of it. As explained in the *Profiles*, John Jennison and David Clarke approached Wild Swan Publications in 1994 with an idea for a survey of the Class 5s that was generally intended to be of principal value to modellers and consisting primarily of tabulated information and detail photographs with extended captions. When David Hunt, Bob Essery and Fred James began work on the *LMS Locomotive Profile* series several years later, the ethos for those works was one of technical drawings and descriptions aimed not only at modellers but also at steam locomotive enthusiasts and historians. Since one of the locomotive types earmarked for coverage in the *Profiles* was the mixed traffic Class 5, the publisher suggested that the two proposals be combined. We decided that this was possible but that the work would have to be produced in three parts if it was to contain the same detail to the same standard as previous *Profiles*. Even then we would not be able to use anywhere near the number of photographs that

we would like from our pooled resources without the size and, therefore, cost growing considerably. This seemed to be a pity, especially for modellers, and so it was resolved to make more of them available in two Photographic Supplements to be published simultaneously with *LMS Locomotive Profiles 5 and 6*.

*Profile No. 5* and its supplement dealt with Nos. 5000–5224 built in 1934 and 1935. *Profile No. 6* and this supplement were originally intended to cover the remaining short-wheelbase locomotives, Nos. 5225–5499 and 4768–4999, but we had a change of heart and extended the coverage to include all the Walschaerts engines and the one Stephenson valve gear example produced from 1936.

Comments, amendments and suggestions will be most welcome and should be addressed to the *Profiles* series editor, David Hunt, who is also responsible for the supplements. This can be by e-mail to *dvhunt@aol.com* or through the parent web site at *www.midlandrecord.com* as well as by post via Wild Swan Publications. From time to time, we publish such material in a 'Further Information' column in *LMS Journal* and will include all that we have had relative to these engines in Part 3 of the Class 5 *Profiles*.

Note that throughout this book, left-hand and right-hand invariably refer to those sides of the locomotive or tender when looking towards the front. This applies despite the orientation of photographs.

*This photograph of 5230 depicts the left-hand side of an Armstrong Whitworth engine as built except for the absence of a crosshead vacuum pump. Features introduced with these locomotives that are visible here included the sloping-throatplate boiler, indicated by the Belpaire corners being above the middle of the intermediate coupled wheel, front smokebox liner plates shown by rivets on the lower part of the door ring, and a hinged smokebox crossbar attached by the two rows of three rivets halfway up the front of the wrapper. From 5225, steam sanding was fitted without hot-water de-sanding, the combination levers had plain lower ends whilst the union links were forked at each end, Derby-style crosshead arms with three-stud fastening were used, and steam-heating pipes were fitted at the front ends. Livery was LMS black, lined vermilion with 1936 block-style numbers and lettering.*

C. TURNER

# INTRODUCTION

*No. 5232 was photographed at Crewe in 1939 and illustrates the right-hand side of an Armstrong Whitworth engine. As well as the differences from earlier Class 5s noted in the previous photograph of 5230, it can be seen here that the tube cleaner cock was mounted higher on the smokebox and there was a support bracket for the door on the right-hand side of the front smokebox ring.*

AUTHORS' COLLECTION

This book is intended primarily to be referred to alongside *LMS Locomotive Profile No. 6*, which contains a detailed discussion of the production and development of the Walschaerts valve gear engines in the 5225–5499 and 4658–4999 series as well as Stephenson gear No. 4767. As with the previous supplement, however, we will give a very brief overview here for readers who do not have that volume.

By the time design of the mixed traffic Class 5 was well advanced, LMS locomotive policy was one of which the main feature was scrap and build. This was officially set out in a report entitled 'Locomotive Construction Policy' dated 20th November 1934 and presented to the LMS Board nine days later. The report stated that in the five years from 1935 to 1939, some 902 locomotives of obsolete design could be replaced by 772 modern locomotives with fifteen classes disappearing. A total of 368 Class 5s would eventually replace 430 old L&NWR locomotives, first priority being to get rid of 144 '19in Goods' engines. The first order was placed as an addition to the 1935 locomotive renewal programme for one hundred Class 5s in place of 108 of the '19in Goods' and twelve other old engines. These locomotives were built by Armstrong Whitworth and were the last of the vertical-throatplate examples covered in the previous supplement.

The Railways (Agreement) Act of 20th December 1935, which made available Government guaranteed loans at low interest rates in order to stimulate industrial recovery from the depression, resulted in both enlargement and acceleration of the programme. In January 1936, the largest single order for locomotives ever placed by a British railway company was also given to Armstrong Whitworth for its Scotswood factory to supply 227 mixed traffic Class 5s, Board approval and confirmation of the order being granted in March. Construction was swift and all were delivered by the end of 1937.

The new locomotives differed from their predecessors in several aspects, those externally apparent being a sloping-throatplate firebox, dome-mounted regulator, steam sanding, and altered combination lever, union link and crosshead arm. Steam heating was restored to the front end, only 25 of the earlier engines having been so equipped.

The building programmes for 1938 and 1939 were much more modest with a total of just 55 Class 5s approved. With over five hundred of them in service, the need for new locomotives was not as great as before and the company's finances were not particularly healthy. In addition, heavy calls were being made on workshop capacity for Government work due to the international crisis and threat of war. In the event, only the twenty engines included in the 1938 programme were actually built when planned, all being turned out from Crewe Works as Nos. 5452–5471 between September and December 1938. These engines incorporated further improvements described later.

Because of altered priorities just before and during the war, the 35 engines in the 1939 building programme weren't actually completed until 1944. Built at Derby, they appeared

Armstrong Whitworth-built No. 5241 was photographed on delivery to Crewe in August 1936. Compared with the other sloping-throatplate locomotives, features characteristic of these engines that can be seen in this study include plain bearing eccentric rod big ends, which were smaller than those on later Class 5s, fitting of crosshead-driven vacuum pumps, cab commode handrails with their lower ends bent through 90 degrees, and single brake blocks. Note the amount of bare, polished metal apparent when the engines were built and the rectangular Armstrong Whitworth makers' plate on the front of the frame. It is apparent from this view that the painting of the cab side was to what had been the Crewe pattern on the vertical-throatplate locomotives with just the front, lower and rear edges lined.

LMS

This photograph was taken at Crewe in 1936 and shows 5421 in photographic grey finish with 1936-style characters. The lining shows up well, that on the cab being again limited to the front, lower and rear edges in what was previously the more restricted Crewe style. There is no doubt that 5421's trailing axle was hollow as we can see right through it.

LMS

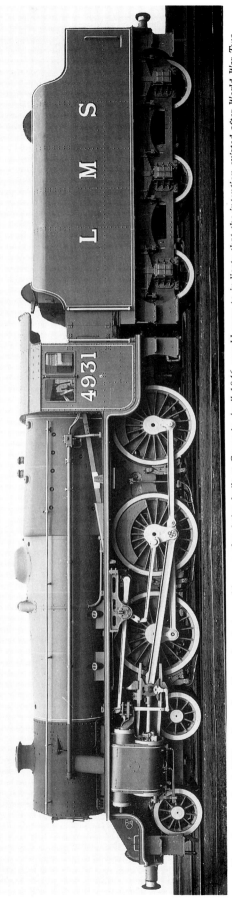

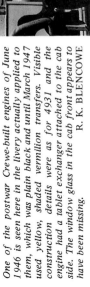

This photograph of 4931, taken when it was in photographic grey after being built at Crewe in April 1946, would seem to indicate that the intention existed after World War Two to return to pre-war lined livery for the Class 5s, albeit with the scroll-and-serif cabside numbers in a higher position. That they were actually painted plain black was explained by the Company Chairman, Sir William Wood, as being due to shortages of paint, painters and cleaners. Some of the changes to the Class 5 design that had taken place since the Armstrong Whitworth engines were built can be seen and included extra washout plugs at the front of the first barrel ring, atomiser steam cock lower down on the smokebox, enlarged circular access cover on the cylinder clothing, and fabricated valve spindle crosshead guide. Also apparent are the longer slidebars and union link with correspondingly shorter connecting rod, absence of vacuum pump, fluted coupling rods, twin brake shoes, fixed forward cab window without wooden frame, flat window beading, and pillar fixing at the lower end of the commode handrail. Close examination also reveals the operating spindle for the hopper ashpan between intermediate and trailing coupled wheels just below the coupling rod and in front of the sand pipe. Although part-welded tenders had been introduced in November 1945, No. 4931 was coupled to a welded one.
AUTHORS' COLLECTION

One of the postwar Crewe-built engines of June 1946 is seen here in the livery actually applied to them, which was plain black and until March 1947 used yellow, shaded vermilion transfers. Visible construction details were as for 4931 and the engine had a tablet exchanger attached to the cab side. The window glass in the cab front appears to have been missing.
R. K. BLENCOWE

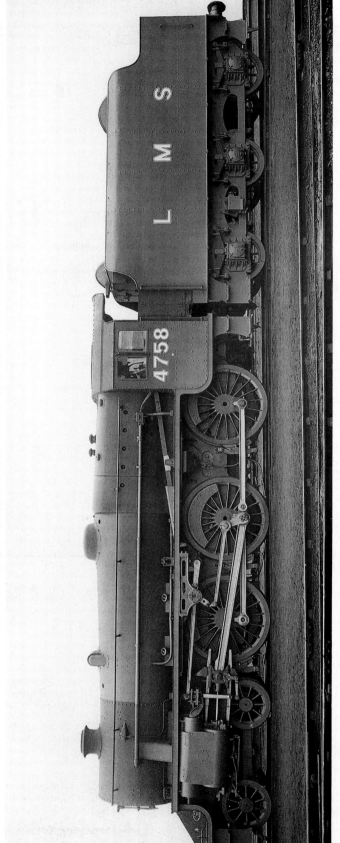

Starting with No. 4997 produced in March 1947, LMS-built Class 5s were turned out in plain black with 1946-pattern straw transfers having maroon edging and inset lining. This photograph of 4768, built at Crewe a month later, shows the engine in photographic grey and illustrates the scheme nicely. Locomotives by this time were being built with self-cleaning smokeboxes, as shown by the SC plate on the smokebox door, and boilers with top feed on the first barrel ring. The top feed design had been changed with simple non-return valve clacks in the middle, hence there were no setscrews protruding from the shoulders. The lack of rivets around the lower part of the smokebox door ring indicates that there were no front liner plates, as was the case with all engines built after this time. The tender was one of the part-welded ones introduced in November 1945 and coupled to the later Class 5s when built and it had external sieve boxes between leading and intermediate axleboxes. Note the rubber extensions to the underside of the gangway doors; these were designed to offer a measure of draught protection as well as preventing lumps of coal from falling off the footplate.

AUTHORS' COLLECTION

In 1947, Ivatt initiated a series of experiments with roller bearings on the axles of some newly-built Class 5s. The first one produced in September that year was 4758, which had Timken bearings to all axles. This and subsequent engines also had extended wheelbases between intermediate and trailing coupled wheels and lengthened smokeboxes, both of which are apparent in this study of 4758 in photographic grey finish. More difficult to discern is the fact that the bogie frames were slightly longer than before and so the life guards projected a little further ahead of the wheels. Later-pattern cylinder drains with vertical valves, altered operating linkage and different diameter pipes were fitted, 4758 being the first engine to have them. The tender also had Timken roller bearing axleboxes with quite distinctive circular covers. Other details were as noted for the earlier 1947 engines and included 1946-style livery. Once again, the rubber gangway door extensions are visible.

LMS

as 5472–5499 and 4800–4806, the numerical step back being occasioned by the 'Patriots' taking the block from 5500 onwards. Once again, the engines incorporated several differences from their predecessors.

Between June and November 1943, another 160 Class 5s were ordered, approval for their construction being granted by the Ministry of Production. They were needed for dealing with long-distance military personnel and stores trains and were built at all three major LMS Locomotive Works in England. Because of this, the first actually to appear was not 4807, which was constructed at Derby, but 4826 from Crewe in July 1944. Another thirty were built at Crewe and Horwich as numbers 4967–4996 between April 1946 and February 1947.

In December 1945, the building programme for 1947 was approved and included 65 Class 5s. By this time, George Ivatt was acting CME and recommended that twenty of them should be fitted with Caprotti valve gear; these engines will be

*Whilst some turntables were vacuum operated, the majority worked on the musclepower of the crew. This view shows Derby-built No. 5477 of July 1943 on a manually-operated table after it had received extra washout plugs at the front of the first barrel ring near the top and had been patch painted with new scroll-and-serif transfers in the higher position on its cab side — a common austerity era occurrence.*
R. K. BLENCOWE

*Built as No. 4906 at Crewe in October 1945, this engine was renumbered by BR in April 1948 and had its new number applied in what appear to have been hand-painted characters. Its smokebox door number plate was one of the relatively few with BR numbers shown in scroll-and-serif style and its tender retained the LMS lettering with which it had been embellished when built. Engine and welded Mk 2 tender were in typical condition for the 4892-4911 batch built to Crewe order 492 with top feed on the second ring of the boiler and short wheelbase.*    REAL PHOTOGRAPHS

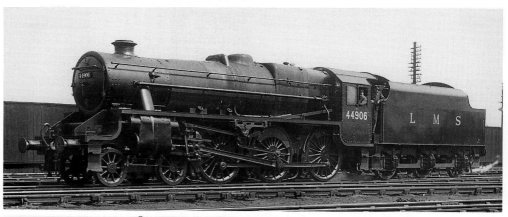

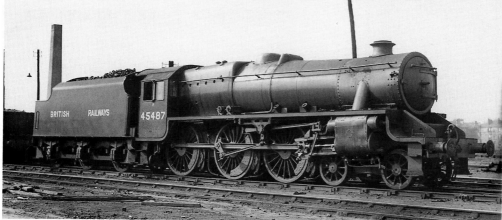

*Another locomotive typical of its series as running immediately after Nationalisation was 45487. Built at Derby in November 1943 as part of O/4141 to Lot 152 comprising Nos. 5482-5496, it was renumbered by British Railways in May 1948 and its tender was lettered to display new ownership, both numbers and letters being hand-painted. It did not have any smokebox door number plate when photographed shortly afterwards. Except for the addition of washout plugs at the front of the first barrel ring, the engine and tender appear to have been unaltered since being built.*
       R. K. BLENCOWE

*Horwich Works built Nos. 4997-4999 and 4783-4799 to order No. 98 of Lot 187 between March and May 1947. Apart from 4783 and 4997, all were fitted with forward top feed boilers but without 'top hat' covers. They also had self-cleaning smokeboxes, hopper ashpans and rocking firegrates, the operating linkage for the latter being visible above the platform alongside the firebox in this view of 44999 at Polmadie. All axles were solid and it can be seen that the trailing one still only had a turning centre rather than being bored through when this picture was taken. The engine was renumbered in June 1948 and repainted at Horwich in early BR lined black livery, probably early in 1949. Like its fellow, the engine had no smokebox liner plates but was fitted with fabricated valve spindle crosshead guides, long slidebars and union links, short connecting rods, fluted coupling rods and twin brake blocks. Its forward cabside windows were fixed without wooden frames, the window beading was flat, and the commode handrails were fixed with pillars at their lower ends. The tender was a part-welded Mk 1 with external sieve boxes. Note that the lining at the front of the platform angle curved down to the buffer beam — this seems to have been a Horwich detail and on locomotives painted elsewhere remained horizontal up to the beam.*
       R. K. BLENCOWE

No. 44658 was the only one of four engines fitted when new with electric lighting that did not also have roller bearing axleboxes. It did, however, have a long wheelbase and smokebox and was fitted with a boiler having the last type of top feed with centre-mounted caged clacks and setscrews protected by a tall cover. It had a self-cleaning smokebox, rocking firegrate, and hopper ashpan, the operating spindle for the latter projecting from below the coupling rod in front of the trailing coupled wheel. Cylinder drain valves and pipes were the later type, the buffer beam had round-head rivets, there were no front smokebox liner plates, and the atomiser steam cock was mounted below the handrail. Valve spindle crosshead guides were fabricated, slidebars and union links were long, whilst connecting rods were short, and coupling rods were fluted. Forward cabside windows were fixed, beading was flat, and handrails had pillars at the lower ends. The tender was a part-welded one with external sieve boxes but plain bearing axleboxes. Livery was the second iteration of BR lined black when the tender lettering had been omitted but there were no emblem transfers available, which puts the repainting date as probably between the middle of 1949 and early 1950.

BRITISH RAILWAYS (LMR)

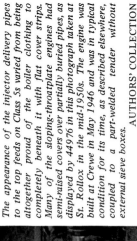

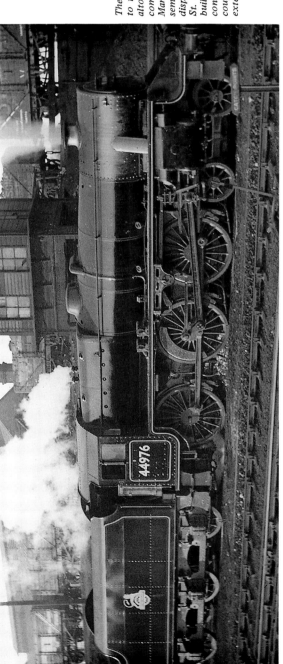

The appearance of the injector delivery pipes to the top feeds on Class 5s varied from being altogether proud of the boiler clothing to completely beneath it with flat cover strips. Many of the sloping-throatplate engines had semi-raised covers over partially buried pipes, as displayed by 44976 in this photograph taken at St. Rollox in the mid-1950s. The engine was built at Crewe in May 1946 and was in typical condition for its time, as described elsewhere, coupled to a part-welded tender without external sieve boxes.

AUTHORS' COLLECTION

*The first engine built during World War Two was 5472, which emerged from Derby Works in April 1943. Compared with pre-war production at Crewe, it was without smokebox front liner plates, had shorter connecting rods but longer slidebars, piston rods and union links, its coupling rods were fluted, and circular access holes and covers in the cylinder clothing were enlarged. There were also many internal and less apparent outside alterations that are comprehensively discussed in the* Profile. *By the time this photograph was taken at St. Rollox in April 1958, it also had extra washout plugs at the front of its boiler, a late-pattern top feed with raised cover, and a solid driving axle. Its original welded tender had been replaced with a riveted one and it was freshly painted in lined BR black livery with 8in cabside numerals, 5MT power classification above the numbers, and post-1956 BR crests on the tender. The crest seen here was one of the early ones produced with a right-facing lion specifically for the right-hand sides of engines and tenders. The College of Heralds, however, pointed out that only left-facing lions had been approved when the design was submitted to them and so after just a few of the incorrect ones had been used, all right-facing transfers were scrapped.*

R. K. BLENCOWE

covered in Part 3 of the Class 5 Profiles. The Walschaerts valve gear examples were built at Crewe and Horwich between March and December 1947 with the first three taking the number sequence to 4999. Another start was therefore made with 4758, which followed on from the Caprotti locomotives, and the sequence was taken up to 4789. The last one built by the LMS was 4767, which was different from all other Class 5s as it had Stephenson valve gear.

The last eighty LMS-designed Class 5s were not actually completed until after Nationalisation. The Walschaerts valve gear engines were constructed at Horwich and Crewe between July 1948 and December 1950 and again the sequence of numbers had to step backwards. Even then, they weren't built in numerical order and the first forty became 44698–44737, British Railways having added 40,000 to their allocated LMS numbers, followed by 44658–44697. A summary of the 595 LMS-designed Class 5s built with sloping-throatplate fireboxes and Walschaerts or Stephenson valve gear is shown in the table.

**Walschaerts and Stephenson valve gear LMS mixed traffic Class 5s built with sloping-throatplate fireboxes**

| Numbers | Makers | Delivered |
|---|---|---|
| 5225–5451 | Armstrong Whitworth | Aug 36–Dec 37 |
| 5452–5461 | Crewe Works | Sep 38–Oct 38 |
| 5462–5471 | Crewe Works | Nov 38–Dec 38 |
| 5472–5481 | Derby Works | Apr 43–Sep 43 |
| 5482–5491 | Derby Works | Sep 43–Dec 43 |
| 5492–5499 4800–4806 | Derby Works | Jan 44–Jul 44 |
| 4807–4825 | Derby Works | Sep 44–Dec 44 |
| 4826–4835 | Crewe Works | Jul 44–Sep 44 |
| 4836–4845 | Crewe Works | Sep 44–Oct 44 |
| 4846–4855 | Crewe Works | Nov 44–Dec 44 |
| 4856–4861 | Crewe Works | Dec 44–Jan 45 |
| 4862–4871 | Crewe Works | Jan 45–Mar 45 |
| 4872–4891 | Crewe Works | Mar 45–Aug 45 |
| 4892–4911 | CreweWorks | Sep 45–Nov 45 |
| 4912–4931 | Crewe Works | Nov 45–Apr 46 |
| 4932–4941 | Horwich Works | Sep 45–Dec 45 |
| 4942–4966 | Horwich Works | Dec 45–Aug 46 |
| 4967–4981 | Crewe Works | Apr 46–Jul 46 |
| 4982–4996 | Horwich Works | Sep 46–Feb 47 |
| 4997–4999 4783–4789 | Horwich Works | Mar 47–May 47 |
| 4790–4799 | Horwich Works | Jun 47–Oct 47 |
| 4768–4782 | Crewe Works | Apr 47–Aug 47 |
| 4758–4767 | Crewe Works | Sep 47–Dec 47 |
| 44698–44717 | Horwich Works | Jul 48–Dec 48 |
| 44718–44737 | Crewe Works | Jan 49–May 49 |
| 44658–44667 | Crewe Works | May 49–Jul 49 |
| 44668–44685 | Horwich Works | Dec 49–Aug 50 |
| 44688–44697 | Horwich Works | Aug 50–Dec 50 |

A thorough discussion of the origins of the class is in *LMS Locomotive Profile No. 5* and a much more detailed account of the production and development of the engines featured in this book can be found in *LMS Locomotive Profile No. 6*. The same two works also contain detailed descriptions of the engines' construction, components and modifications, *Profile No. 6* concentrating mainly on the differences incorporated in the post-5224 series. Therefore, only a very brief overview of the latter will be included here and will concentrate on those aspects that had an effect on the external appearance of the engines. Some other, less noticeable, external details are pointed out in the photograph captions and we would refer readers to the *Profile* for internal ones. Explanations of the construction and working of the various components and fittings, as well as reasons for alterations, are also in the *Profile*.

# LOCOMOTIVES IN DETAIL

As commented in the previous supplement, there was no differentiation between batches of locomotives in permitted loadings and the only practical difference in performance between the various types of boiler was in coal consumption. Even a Class 5 in run-down condition was capable of handling the trains allotted to any other member of the class, although some jobs, such as the prestigious Carlisle fitted freights worked by Saltley crews, would normally have one of the better engines allocated. This selection, however, would depend on the general condition of the engine and not the type of boiler, motion, bearings or any other details of its construction.

Where these details really mattered was in availability, overall economy and working conditions for the men who had to operate and maintain them. Horizontal poppet valves on the cylinder drains were less liable than the vertical type to jam open and affect an engine's performance or require unscheduled maintenance. Monel metal firebox stays were less likely to fracture and require replacement outside the normal repair cycle. The sloping-throatplate boilers used slightly less coal per horsepower/hour at the drawbar and roller bearings and manganese steel axlebox liners extended the mileage between repairs as well as making the engines more comfortable to work on than before. Self-cleaning smokeboxes, rocking grates and hopper ashpans made life less unpleasant for footplate and disposal crews and helped maintain acceptable recruitment levels in the postwar period of full employment and expectations of less arduous working conditions. The majority of the many alterations made to the basic Class 5 design and enumerated in the pages that follow were for one or more of the reasons outlined above. They also often had to do with the availability of materials during the second world war, when output was directed primarily towards the military effort, and in the austerity years that followed when the country was struggling to recover economically and to rebuild.

Since locomotive batches were often ordered and/or produced simultaneously at two or more Works, the sequence in which they were built was not necessarily that in which they were numbered. This

became even more pronounced after the war. Where we indicate a particular engine as being the first to be built with a particular feature, therefore, it cannot be assumed that all *numerically* following would be the same. Rather, it is an indication of the date when the change was introduced and that locomotives following *chronologically* would have it Full lists of the post-5224 engines with their building, numbering, renumber-

ing and other significant dates are included in the *Profile*.

## VARIATIONS AS BUILT

Construction was closely similar to the earlier, vertical-throatplate engines as described in *Profile No. 5* and its associated supplement, so we will concentrate here on the differences from those locomotives and the alterations introduced on succes-

*The front end of Armstrong Whitworth No. 5235 as built in August 1936 is shown here. Points to note include the smokebox door support bracket and rivets at either side of the door ring showing that a hinged crossbar was fitted. The rivets around the lower part of the ring show that front liner plates were incorporated in the smokebox. The buffer beam was flush-riveted, although there were prominent bolt heads at either end, and steam heating was fitted at the front. The smokebox door hinges, straps, locking handles and support bracket were bright metal, whereas those on LMS-built engines were black, and the numberplate had 1936-style sans-serif characters. The engine still lacked a shed code plate when the photograph was taken.*

A. G. ELLIS

Although none of the engines covered in this volume was built with a tall chimney, some could occasionally be seen with them. One such example was 5439, seen at Willesden during the war after its crosshead vacuum pump was removed. Apart from the pump and chimney, the engine bears all the hallmarks of the first 227 sloping-throatplate engines as built that can be seen from this aspect — top feed on the second ring, high mounted atomiser steam cock, steam sanding with no hot-water de-sanding, straight, fluted combination lever with union link forked at each end, Derby-style crosshead arm with three-stud fastening, plain-section coupling rods, small eccentric rod big end, cast valve spindle crosshead guide, single brake blocks, small access cover in cylinder clothing, early-pattern cylinder drain valves, front steam-heating pipe, flush-riveted buffer beam, smokebox front liner plates, hinged smokebox crossbar, smokebox door support bracket, and sliding front windows in the cab side. It was also coupled to a welded Mk 2 tender without external sieve boxes. Note the support bracket at the fronts of the cylinder drain pipes.

AUTHORS' COLLECTION

Many characteristics of the 1946 Horwich engines can be seen in this study of 4984 in charge of an ordinary passenger train, probably in 1948. They include front smokebox liner plates, as shown by the rivets around the lower part of the door ring, round-head rivets on the buffer beam, large access covers in the cylinder clothing, washout plugs at the front of the boiler near the top, long slidebars, piston rod and union link with short connecting rod, fluted coupling rods, large eccentric rod big ends, fabricated valve spindle crosshead guides, solid axles, twin brake blocks, fixed front cabside windows with flat beading, and tenders with part-welded tanks and 'knock back' short spring hangers. The engines also had self-cleaning smokeboxes and although cast 'SC' plates were specified, some early examples had the letters simply painted on the smokebox door, as seen here. No. 4984 was one of four engines we know to have been fitted with Hudd AWS in 1947, as shown by the vacuum reservoir on the platform just in front of the cab. It was also one of the last locomotives to be turned out when built in plain black with scroll-and-serif transfers. Note the scroll-and-serif smokebox door number plate with painted rim.

AUTHORS' COLLECTION

sive batches. The Armstrong Whitworth 5225–5451 series differed from its immediate predecessors in having sloping-throatplate, domed boilers with 24 superheater elements as part of the transition from Stanier's early precepts on low-degree superheating that he had brought from Swindon. They also had steam sanding, which was another departure from Stanier's practice brought from the GWR, and were without hot-water de-sanding. Combination levers were straight and fluted as before but had plain lower ends with both extremities of the union links forked and the crossheads had Derby-style drop arms with three stud fastenings. Carriage-warming hoses were fitted at the front ends and the tube cleaner cocks were mounted higher on the smokebox sides. Smokeboxes had front liner plates, as shown by the rivets around the lower part of the door ring, and hinged crossbars, indicated by the parallel rows of three rivets on either side of the wrapper at the front and adjacent ones on the ring. On the

right-hand side was a door support bracket.

The remaining pre-war locomotives, 5452–5471, were built at Crewe in 1938 with 28-element boilers having a few other internal modifications and the intermediate ashpan doors were omitted. This was because of trouble experienced with ash escaping from the doors getting into the trailing axleboxes and causing them to overheat. The eccentric rod big ends were enlarged and had SKF ball bearings whilst the crosshead-driven vacuum pump was omitted and the 'Dreadnought' brake valve used hitherto was replaced by an LMS standard type. Brake hangers carried twin blocks with fixed heads to extend time between replacement, fixing of the cab commode handrails at their lower ends was altered, and a sand gun was fitted on the firebox backplate. The last ten, 5462–5471, had thicker frame plates, strengthened drag boxes and J hangers with spring links under tension for the coupled wheels, the springs being sixteen rather than ten

plates. The atomiser steam cock on the left-hand side of the smokebox was repositioned below the handrail.

The next batch should have been built in 1939 at Crewe but the war intervened and they were eventually turned out by Derby Works starting with 5472 in April 1943. Their slidebars, union links and piston rods were lengthened and connecting rods shortened so that it was no longer necessary to split the crosshead from the piston rod when withdrawing the piston. Because of wartime restrictions on the availability of specialist steels, the coupling rods were made from lower tensile strength material and were therefore fluted. There were various internal alterations to the boiler and smokebox, the visible difference being the lack of rivet heads around the bottom of the door ring because the front liner plates were omitted. Other differences were in the frames, pistons, bogie and boiler lagging but none was visible from outside. Full details are included in the *Profile*. Two further small changes were enlargement of

*This close-up view shows the left-hand motion of No. 4817, one of the 1943 Derby engines built to O/8263. Immediately obvious are the large eccentric rod big end, hollow axle, and fluted coupling rods — the slight fishbelly profile of the latter being evident above the connecting rod. Further forward can be seen the later style of combination lever with plain lower end and union link having forks at both ends as well as a fabricated valve spindle crosshead guide. The transverse support for the rear end of the motion girder bracket was called the motion plate whilst the forward one was referred to as the slidebar bracket.*
                                                                                                    HMRS (AL434)

the circular access holes in the cylinder clothing and the addition of drain cocks on the injector bodies. From 5492, built in January 1944, two additional washout plugs appeared on top of the first boiler ring just behind the smokebox and the split pins at the tops of the brake hangers were replaced by clips.

The next visible changes occurred on the Crewe and Derby-built locomotives starting with 4826 at Crewe and 4807 at Derby in July and September 1944 respectively (this was a notable instance where numerical sequences did not reflect the modification state of the engines). Apart from alterations to the frames, the valve spindle crosshead guides were fabricated from steel instead of being two-piece iron castings, round-head rivets were used on the buffer beams where previously they had been flush, the front cab side windows were fixed as opposed to sliding and were without wooden frames, and the beading around the cab windows was flat with square lower corners rather than being half-round and radiused at the bottom. This was due to a shortage of half-round strip that was acquired from the Carriage and Wagon Works. Crewe-built locomo-

*This study of 45332 taken in the 1960s illustrates the cab structure of the Armstrong Whitworth engines. The cab windows were both able to slide and were fitted in wooden frames with half-round beading whilst the commode handrails were bent through 90 degrees at the lower end and bolted directly into the wing plates. The locomotive was AWS fitted and had overhead warning flashes. A patch of its very grubby paintwork had been cleaned on the cab side and it appears that new 8in Gill Sans numbers had been applied. The filthy state of many locomotives at this time made it difficult, if not impossible, for signalmen to read engine numbers, which was a requirement of the rule book. Consequently, the practice of cleaning a patch of the cab side and even applying fresh numbers was not uncommon.* AUTHORS' COLLECTION

*This photograph was taken at Stafford in September 1964 and shows the exhaust steam injector below the right-hand side of the cab on No. 45439. By this time, the injector bodies had drain cocks at their lower extremities so that they could be emptied when the engines were standing in very cold weather to avoid them freezing.* R. J. ESSERY

*The second style of cab was that on Nos. 5452-5499 and 4800-4806, shown in this 1960s picture of AWS-fitted 45493. Whilst the forward cabside windows were still the sliding type with wooden frames and the beading was half-round, the lower end of the commode handrail was fixed to a pillar. The tube cleaning cock had been mounted lower down the side of the smokebox than originally with an external feed pipe from a union above the handrail.*

AUTHORS' COLLECTION

*Locomotives numbered from 4807 onwards had the last style of cab (not counting those on the Caprotti engines) although the first to appear with it was Crewe-built 4826. As can be seen in this study of Derby-built No. 4817 of November 1944, as well as altered commode handrail fixing, the cabside windows were modified. The forward one, which in this picture was painted black as a wartime measure, was fixed and had no wooden inner frame whilst the beading was flat and had sharp lower corners. Livery was plain black with yellow, shaded vermilion, numbers and power classification shown simply as '5'.*
*HMRS (AL432)*

*The Manson tablet exchanging apparatus fitted to the left-hand cab side of several Northern Division, later Scottish Region, locomotives is shown in this photograph of 45479. The cab was one of the interim type having sliding front windows on the sides but commode handrail with pillar fixing at the lower end. The power classification appears to have been applied using a transfer '5' but hand-painted 'MT'. Note the rubber extension to the bottom of the gangway door — this was easily damaged and needed frequent replacement, so sometimes it was just cut off below the door and not replaced until the next works visit.*
*P. TATLOW*

tives had front smokebox liner plates, and hence rivets on the door ring, whereas those from Derby did not.

Engines of the 1945 and 1946 production from Crewe and Horwich, 4872–4966, were little changed from those immediately preceding them. Wartime operating conditions, however, highlighted many shortcomings of locomotive detail design and emphasised their labour-intensive nature. As part of the attempts to extend mileage between repairs and reduce manpower requirements for inspection, maintenance and disposal, the majority of these engines had self-cleaning smokeboxes

whilst the last ten from Crewe and the Horwich-built examples from 4942 onwards had rocking grates and hopper ashpans. Tenders coupled to some of these engines also had alterations incorporated as described later.

In March 1947, Horwich Works introduced another two visible alterations. Starting with No. 4997, the smokebox front liner plates were omitted again, marked by the absence once more of rivets at the bottom of the door ring. The next engine, 4998, also had a different design of top feed with simplified clacks housed in the centre casting so there were

no setscrews projecting above the shoulders. The top feed was also moved forwards to the first ring of the boiler.

In September 1947, the first Class 5 with roller-bearing axleboxes – No. 4758 – appeared and eventually 37 of them were built with Walschaerts valve gear and roller bearings either on the driving axle alone or on all axles. There was also the unique 4767 with roller bearings to all axles and Stephenson valve gear. Bearings were made by Timken and by SKF. Details of which engines had which bearings on which axles can be found in the *Profile*. The wider horngaps required for roller bearings

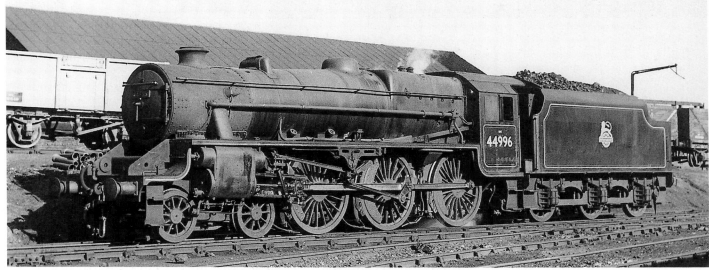

*Eastfield in June 1956 was the setting for this study of 44996. The forward top feed boiler with raised cover over the clacks had been fitted in May 1954 and the original part-welded tender replaced by a welded type. Livery was the St. Rollox version of lined black with plain cylinder clothing bands and 10in cabside numbers. Power classification was 5MT and the tender sides carried 'monocycling lions'. Having been built at Horwich in February 1947, the engine had fluted coupling rods, enlarged ball-bearing eccentric rod big ends, long slidebars, union link and piston rod, and fabricated valve spindle crosshead guide. It also had a hopper ashpan, the operating spindle for which can just be seen between intermediate and trailing coupled wheels below the coupling rod.*

AUTHORS' COLLECTION

*From No. 4942 built at Horwich in December 1945, Class 5s were fitted when new with fireboxes having hopper ashpans so that the fire could be dropped and ash cleaned out without someone having to go under the engine with a rake. The hopper mechanism was controlled by a spindle jutting out between the left-hand intermediate and trailing coupled wheels, as shown here. To operate it, a long handle that was normally stowed beneath the fireman's seat would be slotted on to the short lever at the end of the spindle. The pin seen secured to the mounting bracket by a chain would be removed from its housing and the locking catch rotated. The operating handle could then be turned through 90 degrees, which would open the hopper doors in the bottom of the ashpan. It was essential to open the doors before dropping the fire through the rocking grate, which was also fitted to these engines, or the heat could distort and jam them. Also evident in this view is the later type of brake hanger with twin brake blocks and fixed heads.*

D. J. CLARKE

*Three locomotives were built with both double chimneys and electric lighting, one of them being No. 4766 seen here shortly after being turned out from Crewe in December 1957. Its boiler had the top feed mounted on the first barrel ring but since the clacks were the simple non-return valve type, there were no setscrews and therefore no extended 'top hat' cover. Cylinder drain valves were the later, vertical type with different diameter pipes and operating linkage from the cab only to the outer ones. The engine also had an extended wheelbase and all axles were fitted with Timken roller bearings, as were those on the part-welded tender with circular axlebox covers. Livery was 1946 LMS-style unlined black with straw, sans-serif cabside numbers and tender letters that were edged maroon and had inset maroon lining. The tender was fitted with external sieve boxes.*
AUTHORS' COLLECTION

meant that the firebox had to be moved 4in to the rear, so the wheelbase between driving and trailing wheels was increased by the same amount, as was the length of the smokebox. Contrary to what has been suggested in other publications, the cabs of the long-wheelbase engines were not extended but were exactly the same length as all the others. To simplify marking and cutting out of plates, all subsequent Class 5s had the same dimensions whether or not they had roller bearings. No. 4758 also introduced a new type of cylinder drain cock and altered linkage, only the two outer cocks being operated from the cab and the centre one from the steam chest being automatic. Drain pipes from the cylinder cocks were ¼in thicker than before whereas the middle one was ⅛in narrower and was routed behind the others. Three of the engines, 4765–4767, were built with double blastpipes and chimneys. Later trials of different chimney and blastpipe arrangements with 4765, however, showed no practical advantage.

The last external alteration to Class 5 production, apart from Caprotti valve gear, occurred when 44698 was built at Horwich in July 1948 with another pattern of top feed in which clack cages retained by enlarged caps with standard clamping setscrews were used. They were mounted in the centre of the later type of casting, however, and a raised 'top hat' cover was incorporated to cover the setscrews.

From the above, it can be seen that there were many more variations in the sloping-throatplate engines as built than with their vertical-throatplate predeces-

*Another Hudd AWS-fitted engine was Kentish Town-based 44822, seen here shortly after being renumbered in May 1948 wearing plain black livery with 8in cabside numbers and a relatively unusual scroll-and-serif smokebox door numberplate with painted rim. This engine was part of the 1943 Derby production that had flush-riveted buffer beam and no front smokebox liner plates. It was one of the first to have washout plugs at the front of the barrel at the top but one of the last with cast valve spindle crosshead guides. Like all post-1938 locomotives, its coupling rods were fluted.*
R. K. BLENCOWE

sors. Many of the improvements that were introduced over the years were also incorporated into earlier locomotives as they passed through the Works, or even at running sheds, whereas others were not. Those that were carried out retrospectively often took many years to affect the entire stock and others never did. Thus, the combination of features to be seen on any particular engine could vary quite markedly from its neighbour on shed or out on the road. Fairly comprehensive details of all these alterations, the engines

that received them and the dates on which they were carried out are given in the *Profile*. Here we will content ourselves with pointing out in photograph captions some of those apparent on various locomotives.

## AWS

Nos. 4822, 4846, 4984 and 5267 received Hudd equipment for operating over the London, Tilbury & Southend Section of the LMS in 1947. A brief history and description of the Hudd system as used on the LT&S was given in *LMS Locomotive Profile*

*No. 5468 was built at Crewe in December 1938 as part of Order No. 406 to Lot 142. It was intended that these engines should be equipped from new with BTH speed indicators and, as can be seen in this c.1939 photograph, a bracket for the alternator was fitted outside the left-hand trailing wheel. As far as we are aware, however, No. 5468 never received the indicating equipment. Differences between this engine and the 227 Armstrong Whitworth locomotives that are visible in this picture are a larger eccentric rod big end, twin brake blocks, no vacuum pump, repositioned atomiser steam cock, and altered lower fixing of the cab commode handrails with a pillar rather than 90 degree bend. Livery was lined black with scroll-and-serif, countershaded transfers plus scroll-and-serif smokebox door numberplate. Note that when the photograph was taken, the circular access covers in the cylinder clothing were still small and the front ends of the cylinder drain pipes were still supported by a bracket attached to the cover.*                                                    *R. K. BLENCOWE*

*Another Armstrong Whitworth locomotive, No. 45262, is seen in this photograph, possibly taken at York, sometime after it was fitted with a speed indicator in November 1961. As well as having a speed indicator, the engine was AWS fitted — a relatively rare combination for a Class 5. Since the locomotive was built in October 1936, the crosshead vacuum pump had been removed, the atomiser steam cock on the smokebox had been moved to below the handrail, the circular access covers in the cylinder clothing had been enlarged, and later-pattern top feed and cover had been fitted. The photograph illustrates the earlier type of sliding front cabside window with wooden frame, half-round window beading, lower fixing of the commode handrail, and small eccentric rod big end with plain bearings. Livery was standard lined BR black with overhead warning flashes. Note the evidence of leakage from the Mk 2 welded tender tank — a perennial problem with these tenders that led to the introduction of part-welded ones.*                    AUTHORS' COLLECTION

*No. 5.* After the war, the Hudd system was developed into the BR Automatic Warning System described in *LMS Locomotive Profile No. 4 – The Princess Royals.* It was first fitted to a Class 5 when No. 44911 received it at Doncaster Works in April 1956. During the rest of that year and early in 1957, the locomotive was stationed at King's Cross to test the equipment on the AWS-equipped East Coast Main Line. After the trials were over, most Class 5s received AWS equipment, details of those we know being in the *Profile.*

### SPEED INDICATORS

In 1936, Nos. 5264 and 5278 were fitted with Hasler indicators and recorders for high-speed tests on the Midland Division. It was then intended that all new Class 5s would have BTH speed indicators and existing locomotives would be fitted with them as they passed through the shops. Problems with the equipment and the outbreak of war, however, severely curtailed the programme and we know of only 76 of the engines featured in this supplement that were fitted between 1938 and 1941. Difficulty in obtaining spares and maintaining the equipment under wartime condi-

*As remarked elsewhere, not many Class 5s were fitted with both AWS and speed indicators, No. 45272 being among the few of which we are aware. The alternator for the Smith-Stone speed indicator can be seen on the return crank, steadied by an armoured cable leading to a wheel size adjustment rheostat box supported by a bracket from the platform. An armoured flexible cable led from the rheostat box into the cab. The conduit clipped to the platform angle contained a cable leading from the AWS receiver at the front of the engine to the cab and the small cylinder on top of the platform was the timing reservoir. The locomotive was built by Armstrong Whitworth in November 1936 and originally had coupled axle springs in compression. A close study of the photograph, however, reveals that it had been modified to have 'mutton chop' hangers, one of which can be seen between the spokes at the front of the wheel, with tensioned hangers. Note the single brake block. The photograph was taken at Saltley in July 1964.*                    R. J. ESSERY

## G28627 – Arrangement of No. 6 snowplough

*Drawn at St. Rollox, this shows the later type of plough fitted to the Class 5s and described in the text as well as the alterations to the locomotive necessary for it to be attached.*

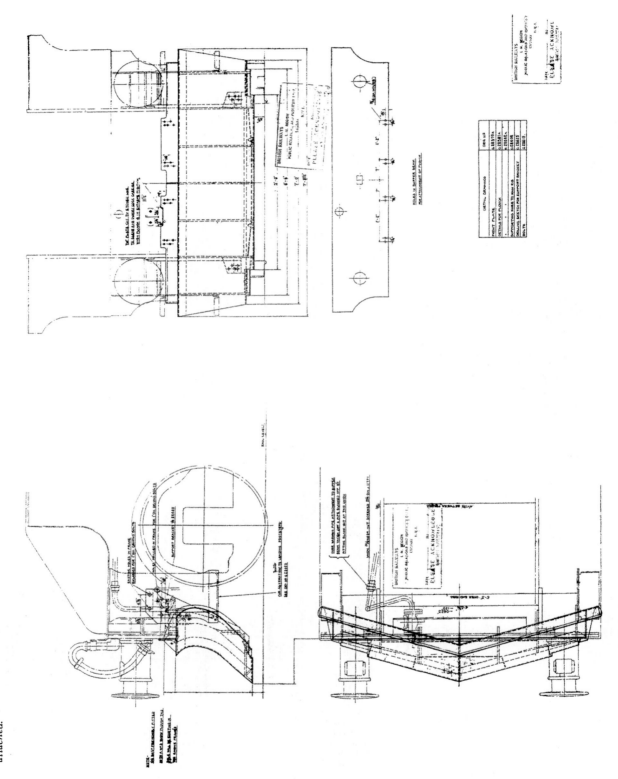

tions led to the CME directing in June 1944 that the instruments, together with all ancillary equipment, should be removed.

In 1949, further trials with various types of speed indicators were carried out but it wasn't until 1960 that any of our present subjects were recorded as being fitted with Smith-Stone equipment. From then until 1963 we know of 78 that were altered before the job was cancelled owing to the accelerated pace of steam engine withdrawal. A description of the Smith-Stone installation is in *LMS Locomotive Profile*

No. 5 and details of the post-5224 engines fitted are in *Profile No. 6*.

## SNOW PLOUGHS

Many Class 5s, particularly Scottish-based ones, were altered so that they could have small snowploughs attached to their front buffer beams in winter. The ploughs were not intended for major snow clearance but to enable trains to run through small drifts up to 2ft deep and to prevent build-up of snow during periods of sparse traffic. Two types were used on Class 5s – the LMS

No. 5 plough and a BR version known as the No. 6. The No. 5 ploughs remained in use after introduction of the No. 6, however, and both types could be seen fitted to Class 5s in the 1950s and 1960s.

Details of the engines in the 5000–5224 number range fitted for ploughs are given in *Profile No. 5* and for the subjects of this volume in *Profile No. 6*. The latter also contains details of the modifications needed to enable engines to take either type of plough.

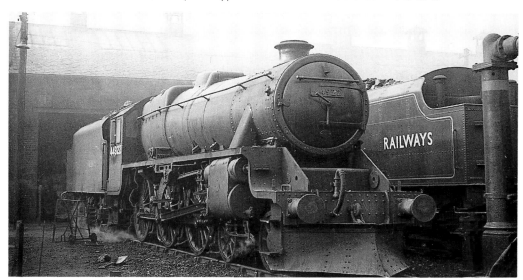

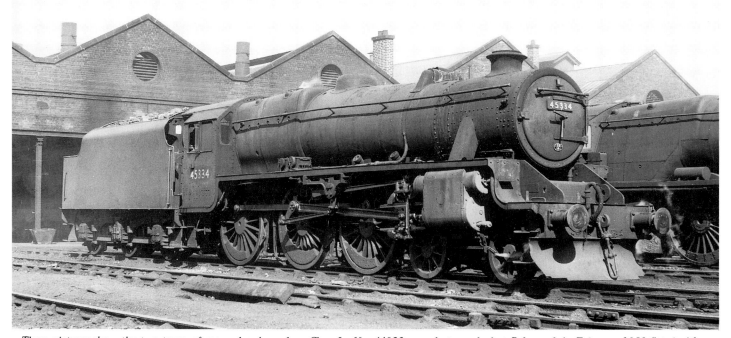

*These pictures show the two types of snow plough used on Class 5s. No. 44922 was photographed at Balornock in February 1950 fitted with a No. 5 plough made by the LMS from an ex-Caledonian design and attached to the buffer beam by two vertical angle-irons. No. 45344 was seen at Carlisle Kingmoor in March 1962 with one of the BR-designed No. 6 ploughs fixed to the buffer beam by a row of bolts along the bottom edge. Note that 45344 had two shed code plates — one on its smokebox door in the usual place and one on the buffer beam just above the plough between the coupling hook and the left-hand buffer. Whether this was to indicate that the plough belonged to Kingmoor we have not been able to determine.*
                                                                    H. C. CASSERLEY and N. E. PREEDY

In July 1954, No. 45389 of Perth shed was photographed at Ferryhill without its front steam-heating hose, which had been removed for servicing during the summer months. As was common on Scottish Region engines, it was fitted with mounting brackets below the buffer beam for a No. 5 snow plough together with fixing holes in the buffer beam and rebates in the front edge of the platform. Since being built by Armstrong Whitworth at Scotswood in July 1937, it had received a forward top feed boiler in February 1953, which type it was destined to retain until March 1958, with washout plugs at the front of the first ring. As with 44978 and several other Scottish Region engines, although it had the last type of top feed with protruding setscrews in the centre, the cover was one of the earlier, low variety through which the setscrews protruded. The cylinder drain pipes were still supported at their front ends by a bracket attached to the cover and the originally flush-riveted buffer beam had been refitted following repair using round-head rivets. Some features of the early sloping-throatplate engines apparent in this view include the cast valve spindle crosshead guide, plain-section coupling rods, eccentric rod big end with plain bearings, half-round cabside window beading, and wooden-framed forward window.

REAL PHOTOGRAPHS

Only a few of the engines covered in this supplement ever carried vertical-throatplate boilers. One such was 45433, which is seen here at the head of a Class D express freight train carrying a 21-element, domeless boiler with transverse-style top feed cover that was probably fitted in March 1955. Apart from the change of boiler type, the engine featured many of the 'standard' alterations seen on Armstrong Whitworth products in the 1950s including repositioned atomiser steam cock and absence of vacuum pump.                    T. G. HEPBURN

Another of the engines originally built with a sloping-throatplate boiler that later carried a vertical-throatplate, 21-element, domeless one, was 45461, which is seen here at the head of the Bon Accord between Glasgow and Aberdeen in the early 1950s. The locomotive had several typically Scottish Region features such as 10in cabside numbers set high to clear the Manson tablet exchanger as well as brackets for the fitting of a No. 5 snow plough together with bolt holes in the buffer beam and rebated front platform.          T. G. HEPBURN

No. 4766 was renumbered 44766 by BR in May 1948 and was photographed wearing its new number at Rugby in May 1949. It still had electric lighting fitted, the Stones turbo generator for which can be seen by the rear of the smokebox behind the steam pipe. Its number had been applied in 10in 1946-style characters without lining or edging that were set midway between the platform and the cab windows but the tender still carried LMS lettering and the smokebox door numberplate was scroll-and-serif. The engine appears to have been unaltered since being built.                                                                B. W. ANWELL

In June 1954, the electric lighting was removed from 44766 and the engine is seen here in its final BR condition at Stafford. Locomotive and tender had been painted in lined BR livery with Gill Sans numbers on smokebox door and cab sides as well as the later style of BR crest on its tender. The only other changes noticeable were that its top feed clacks had been altered to the caged type with the setscrews protected by a 'top hat' cover and it had been fitted with AWS.                                                            G. W. SHARPE

## ELECTRIC LIGHTING

Four of the later engines, 4765–4767 and 44658, were fitted with electric lighting. The LMS equipment consisted merely of electric headlamps, gauge lamps in the cab and inspection lamps above the valve gear. The headlamps were in the usual lamp iron positions on the front platform and there was one on top of the smokebox. Normal lamp irons were also provided inboard of the outer lamps, to the left of the centre one, and on the smokebox door in the cus-tomary position. The system was powered by a Stones steam turbo-generator mount-ed on the right-hand side of the smokebox behind the steam pipe. Later, white indica-tor discs were used on the lamp irons during the day. Unfortunately, the system proved unreliable and was removed between April 1951 and June 1954.

## OIL BURNING

In June 1946, the Ministry of Fuel and Power instigated a scheme to save coal by encouraging large-scale consumers to switch to oil burning if possible. The scheme never reached proper fruition and only five Class 5s were modified. Details of the modification and fixed installations, as well as further information on the whole initiative, are in the *Profile*. To indicate their status, the oil-burning engines had a small 'x' painted on each cab side just below the numbers. By April 1948, the scheme was over and the engines were re-converted to burn coal.

*This view of the front end of 44658 illustrates admir-ably details of one of the last ten Crewe-built engines. The first point to note is that whilst the buffer beam was liberally provided with round-head rivets, it was attached to the platform angle by two domed, hexagon-head bolts at each end. The later type of vertical poppet valve cylinder drains can clearly be seen with only the two outer valves controlled from the cab linkage and the automatic centre valve having a smaller diameter drain pipe routed behind the others. The larger type of cylinder clothing circular access cover is obvious. The engine was one of the few fitted with a Stones turbo generator, seen behind the cylinder steam pipe, and electric lighting. Note that there were normal lamp holders adjacent to each electric head lamp, the upper one being in the normal position on the smokebox door with the electric light on the rim above it. The engine had just been built when the picture was taken and was in immaculate lined BR black livery with Gill Sans smokebox door numberplate. Note the BR style of makers' plate and the red lining on either side of the cylinder clothing bands — St. Rollox did not always apply this to repainted engines. The locomotive was still await-ing a shed code plate but had an 'SC' plate indicating that it was fitted with a self-cleaning smokebox.*
BRITISH RAILWAYS

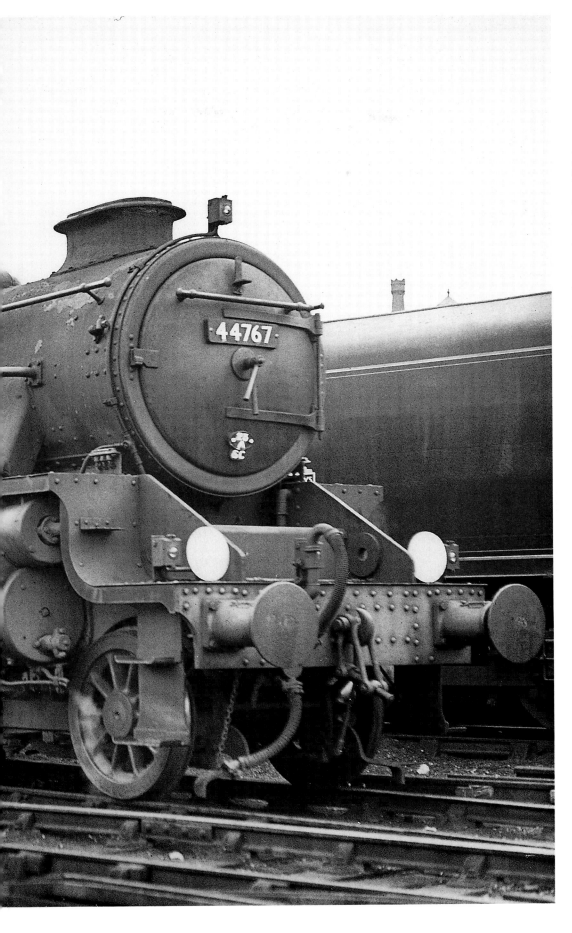

As well as being the only Class 5 to have Stephenson valve gear, No. 4767 was a 27ft 6in wheelbase engine fitted with Timken roller bearings to all axles, electric lighting, and a double blastpipe and chimney. Built in December 1947 at Crewe, it also had many of the later Class 5 features such as the vertical cylinder drain valves with altered operating linkage and pipework, top feed mounted on the first ring of the boiler with no projecting setscrews, self-cleaning smokebox, and rocking firegrate with operating linkage outside the right-hand side of the firebox above the platform, all of which can be seen in this view. Other points worth noting include the facts that its buffer beam had round-head rivets, there were no front smokebox liner plates, valve spindle crosshead guides were fabricated, and connecting rods were short, whilst slide-bars, union links and piston rods were long. Twin brake blocks with fixed heads were fitted, coupling rods were fluted, forward cab windows were fixed and without wooden frames, window beading was flat with sharp lower corners, and the commode handrails had pillar fixings at their lower ends. Because of the bigger axle-boxes and consequently wider horngaps, the bogie frames were longer and so the life guards projected further ahead of the wheels than on plain-bearing bogies. The part-welded tender had Timken roller bearings and external sieve boxes. Drive for the mechanical lubricators was by a rod attached to the rear of the right-hand back gear eccentric rod. Originally turned out in LMS 1946-style livery, the only alteration by the time this picture was taken was that its BR number, applied in April 1948, was shown in 10in sans-serif characters on the cab sides and on a new smokebox door plate. Note the white indicator discs used during the day on the electrically-lit engines after a short time in service.

NATIONAL RAILWAY
MUSEUM
(RANSOME-WALLIS)

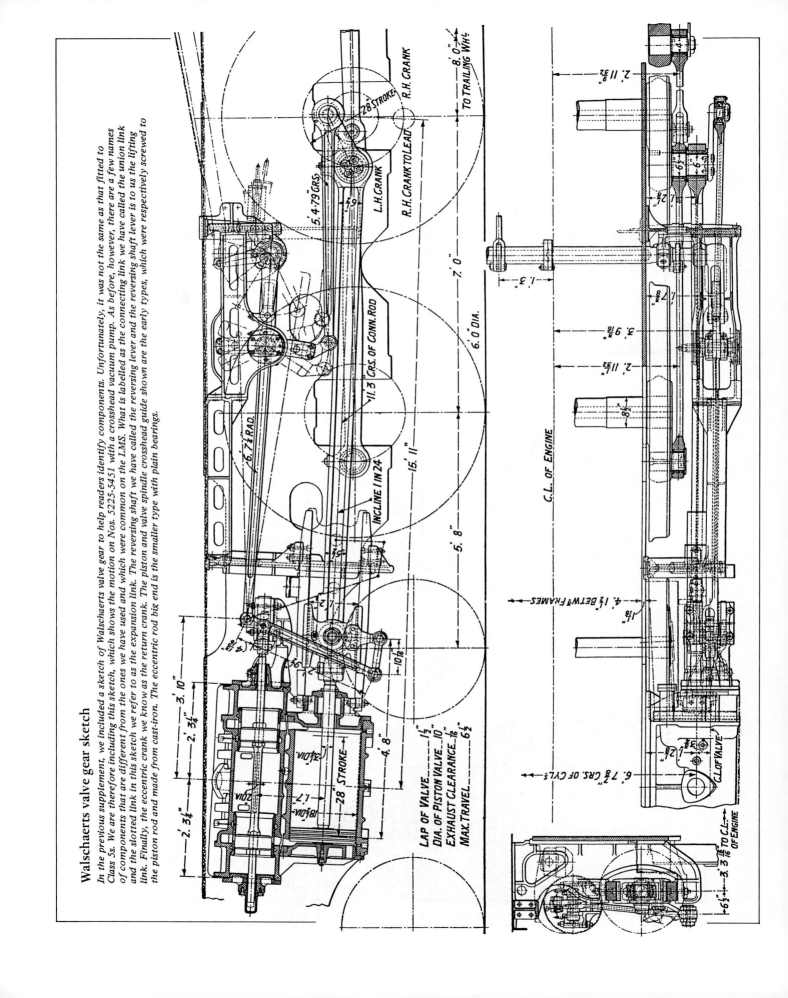

## Walschaerts valve gear sketch

In the previous supplement, we included a sketch of Walschaerts valve gear to help readers identify components. Unfortunately, it was not the same as that fitted to Class 5s. We are therefore including this sketch, which shows the motion on Nos. 5225-5451 with a crosshead vacuum pump. As before, however, there are a few names of components that are different from the ones we have used and which were common on the LMS. What is labelled as the connecting link we have called the union link and the slotted link in this sketch we refer to as the expansion link. The reversing shaft we have called the reversing lever and the reversing shaft lever is to us the lifting link. Finally, the eccentric crank we know as the return crank. The piston and valve spindle crosshead guide shown are the early types, which were respectively screwed to the piston rod and made from cast-iron. The eccentric rod big end is the smaller type with plain bearings.

*This photograph shows No. 44767. Details of the engine are given in the caption on page 29.*

*The Stephenson valve gear fitted to 4767 is shown in detail in this photograph taken just after the engine was built at Crewe. A description of the operation of Stephenson gear and an arrangement drawing of it as fitted to 4767 is in* LMS Locomotive Profile No. 6.

# TENDER VARIATIONS

All the pre-war and many of the wartime engines were coupled when new to Mk. 2 tenders with welded tanks, which were described and illustrated in *LMS Locomotive Profile No. 5* and its associated photographic supplement. Starting with tender No. 10471 first attached to locomotive number 4846 in November 1944, shorter spring links were used with the top pins fitting into deeper shoes than before. The ends of the springs had single pins at the lower ends securing them to modified frame brackets and the arrangement became known as 'knock back hangers'. All subsequent tenders, whether fitted with plain or roller bearing axleboxes, had this type of link.

The main advantages of welded tanks were lighter weight and lower cost. There were, however, leakage problems with some seams so a part-welded version was produced. The first Class 5 to have one was No. 4912 of Crewe Works in November 1945. They could be identified by the absence of horizontal lines of rivet heads immediately above the base and at tank-top level as well as having shorter, rectangular cross-section vents welded to the rear of the hind bulkhead. This type of

tender was rather confusingly referred to in LMS documents as Type 1 or Mark I, which was also the designation of the original all-riveted version.

In March 1947, part-welded tender No. 10670, built at Horwich Works and paired with engine No. 4997, was the first to have external sieve boxes on the frames between leading and intermediate wheels. Those first coupled to locomotives having roller bearings to all axles, Nos. 10640–10649 and 10818–10827, also had roller bearings, which could be identified by their circular axlebox covers.

Four other types of tender were coupled to engines included in this book. Tender No. 9000, which was rebuilt in 1935 from one of the original three 4,000 gallon straight-sided tenders and described in *LMS Locomotive Profile No. 5*, ran with three of them at various times. No. 45329 was recorded as being coupled to a 3,500 gallon Stanier tender from February 1964. As described fully in the *Profile*, construction of a special 3,500 gallon test train tender was commenced at Crewe in 1937 but was then completed at Derby. It had a corridor, vestibule connection, cable duct for connecting test equipment to a

*From March 1946 until June 1958, No. 5298/45298 ran with tender No. 9000, which had been rebuilt in 1935 from one of the original three 4,000-gallon straight-sided tenders initially paired with 'Princess Royal' Pacific No. 6201. It was closely similar to a standard Mk 1 tender, although the curve at the top of the side plates differed slightly at the rear and the rivet pattern on the sides was slightly different at the front. Additionally, tenders Nos. 9000 and 9002 were the only fully-riveted examples to have Timken roller bearing axleboxes with their distinctive covers. Engine and tender had just been repainted in unlined 1946-style LMS livery with 12in high cabside numerals and 14in tender letters when the photograph was taken. For some reason, there was a three-link coupling at the front in place of the screw coupling usually carried. The 8A shed code plate indicates that the locomotive was stationed at Edge Hill.*
*R. J. ESSERY*

dynamometer car, and divided coal space for weighing purposes. It ran with various locomotives during its time as a test vehicle including five Class 5s during trials in 1954. Originally painted crimson lake, it was later black with mixed traffic lining and BR emblems. In 1959 it was rebuilt with a normal, part-welded 4,000 gallon tank and

ran from December that year behind Class 5 No. 45235.

Two coal-weighing tenders were built for test and training purposes in 1946 and a further two appeared in 1950. They were quite different in appearance from standard Stanier tenders and had bunkers that could be weighed by means of side beams

and steelyards. By 1960, the steelyards and their covers had been removed and fire iron tunnels added on the right-hand sides, after which the four tenders were regarded as common pool items. Details of the construction and use of these tenders as well as the Class 5s to which they were attached are in the *Profile*.

*Up to November 1945, sloping-throatplate engines were coupled when built to Mk 2 welded tenders of the type seen in this October 1964 photograph of 45284 at Edge Hill MPD. They had tall, mushroom vents on the rear of the tank, no visible rivets, plain bearing axleboxes with cruciform ribs cast into the covers, and long spring links. When pictured, the engine's top feed cover had been removed and a fitter was attending to the feed mechanism. Livery was lined black with post-1956 crests and overhead warning flashes had been applied, although the single one at the back of the tender was unusual — more commonly there were two positioned above the upper footsteps.*
R. J. ESSERY

*This close-up of the welded tank Mk 2 tender coupled to 45272 at Saltley in July 1964 shows details of the long-pattern spring links fitted prior to November 1944. Also visible are some details of the brake gear as well as the water scoop and operating linkage.* R. J. ESSERY

*Part-welded Mk 1 tenders were readily identifiable by the rivet pattern on the sides. Compared with the fully-riveted variety, the absence of horizontal lines of rivet heads immediately above the base and at tank top level are apparent in this view of 44762 at Willesden in August 1965. Also visible is the left-hand of the short, rectangular cross-section vents that were welded to the rear of the bulkhead in place of the earlier mushroom type. No. 44762 was built at Crewe in October 1947 with Timken roller bearings on all axles including those on its tender. The distinctive circular covers to the tender axleboxes can be seen quite clearly, as can the external sieve box mounted on the frame between leading and intermediate ones. Positioning of the overhead warning flashes just above and inboard of the top steps was typical. Note that the engine was fitted with AWS.*
*R. J. ESSERY*

*Just before locomotive No. 45212 was withdrawn in 1968, it was coupled to a part-welded Mk 1 tender with external sieve boxes, the right-hand one of which is seen in this view. The photograph was taken after the engine and tender had been restored following withdrawal and the top and bottom pieces of angle-iron connected by a long bolt on the outside of the box was added at that stage — it was not a standard feature of BR tenders. Also evident are the later type of 'knock-back' hangers and short spring links.*
*D. J. CLARKE*

*The first part-welded tenders coupled to Class 5s prior to March 1947 did not have external sieve boxes and those attached to engines not having roller bearings were fitted with plain axleboxes. Both these features are apparent on 44952's tender in this picture taken at Carstairs, as are the shorter spring links and fixings with which all part-welded tenders were equipped. The engine had been fitted with AWS and painted at St. Rollox in fully-lined livery with 10in numerals. Post-1956 crests had been applied to the tender.*
AUTHORS' COLLECTION

*Several Class 5s were coupled at various times to the four 3,750-gallon coal weighing tenders. From October 1946 right through to December 1963, No. 4986/44986 was paired with tender 10590, which was one of the two built in 1946 with 8-ton bunkers. They are seen together in this April 1955 photograph taken on the Lickey Incline between Bromsgrove and Blackwell.*　　　　R. C. RILEY

The other 1946 coal weighing tender, No. 10591, ran from June 1958 to November 1967 behind No. 45298. This photograph, believed to have been taken at Shrewsbury and probably shortly after engine and tender left Crewe Works following repair in May 1960, shows them freshly painted with BR heraldic crests and overhead electrification warning flashes. Although we have enumerated alterations to Class 5s over the years elsewhere, it is probably worth examining those visible in this excellent study. Built in December 1936 at Scotswood, the engine had retained its flush-riveted buffer beam and Armstrong Whitworth makers' plate on the front of the frame. The smokebox had received extra side liner plates, as shown by the rivets on the wrapper, and the atomiser steam cock shut-off valve had been moved down to below the handrail. The top feed was still on the second barrel ring but was of the later pattern with centrally-mounted clacks and 'top hat' cover. The bracket supporting the fronts of the cylinder drain pipes had been removed, as had the vacuum pump, and the circular access covers in the cylinder clothing had been enlarged. Livery was fully-lined BR black and included red lining on the cylinder clothing bands. Note the short slidebars and union link, cast valve spindle crosshead guide, wooden-framed forward cabside window, half-round window beading and commode handrail with lower end bent through 90 degrees that were characteristic features of these engines.
AUTHORS' COLLECTION

As far as we are aware, only one engine was ever coupled to a Stanier 3,500-gallon tender. We don't have a photograph of that particular combination but the tender involved, No. 4634, is shown in this picture with 'Jubilee' No. 45651 Shovel, to which it was coupled throughout the life of that engine. It is recorded as having gone to Class 5 No. 45329 from February 1964.
D. HAWKINS

# COMPARISONS AND CONTRASTS

As in our previous photographic supplement, we are using this section to highlight some of the differences between locomotives from the various batches to provide readers with an idea of some details to look for when studying pictures of the class. We have alluded to these changes in other sections but here we will concentrate on six particular engines to make the point. It must also be remembered that

*This study taken at Aviemore shows No. 5470 almost in its original state as built at Crewe Works in December 1938, the only modification apparent being enlargement of the circular access covers in the cylinder clothing. Of the visible differences enumerated in the text between these engines and the Armstrong Whitworth ones, the repositioned atomiser steam cock, absence of a vacuum pump, enlarged eccentric rod big ends for ball bearings, and twin brake blocks can be seen. The engine had been repainted or, at least, patch painted during the later war years and had 10in yellow, shaded vermilion cabside numbers in the high position. It was fitted for the attachment of a No. 5 snow plough with vertical rows of bolt holes in the buffer beam, brackets below it, and rebates in the front of the platform as well as having a Manson tablet exchanger on its cab side.* R. K. BLENCOWE

*In August 1952, No. 45470 was again photographed at Aviemore. The previous October it had been fitted with a later-pattern boiler having the top feed on the first barrel ring and although the central clacks had been altered to the caged type with setscrews, it did not have a 'top hat' cover. During a previous repair its buffer beam had been refitted using round-head rivets. It still had a front support bracket to the cylinder drain pipes and was coupled to the same type of Mk 2 welded tender. Livery was BR lined black with a St. Rollox hallmark of 10in cabside numbers and the tender bore the first style of BR emblem.* AUTHORS' COLLECTION

*No. 5473 was built in May 1943 at Derby with a boiler having the top feed on the second barrel ring. Characteristics of the series apparent in this May 1951 photograph taken at Balornock include the absence of front smokebox liner plates and enlarged circular access covers in the cylinder clothing. Comparison with pictures of earlier engines shows the shorter connecting rods and longer piston rods, slidebars and union links, whilst the fluted coupling rods are clearly seen. The extra washout plugs on the first barrel ring near the top were a later addition. Engine and tender were plain black with an early style of BR livery in which both cabside numbers and tender lettering were applied using 10in characters, the former being halfway between the line of the platform and the cab windows with power classification 5 below.*
AUTHORS' COLLECTION

*By August 1963, No. 45473 had been fitted with a boiler having its later-pattern top feed on the first ring and although it featured caged clacks with setscrews, there was no raised 'top hat' cover. This photograph was taken at Dundee in September 1966 and shows the engine with AWS and a tablet exchanger. Its top lamp holder had been moved to a lower position on the left-hand side of the smokebox door and it was coupled to a riveted tender, having been paired when built with a welded one. The tender sides carried the post-1956 BR crests and the engine's smokebox door numberplate had a painted rim, which was a fairly common embellishment.*
G. HARROP

locomotives built to the same Order or Lot number soon began to display variations, some of which were quite subtle while others were strikingly obvious.

The six locomotives featured are:

No. 5470 built in December 1938 at Crewe. This was the penultimate pre-war engine and featured all the differences from the Armstrong Whitworth locomotives introduced since September 1938. Visible alterations were enlarged eccentric rod big ends for ball bearings, different attachment of the cab commode handrails at their lower ends, omission of the crosshead-driven vacuum pump, fitting of twin brake blocks with fixed heads, and repositioned atomiser steam shut-off cock.

The coupled axle spring links were fitted under tension to 'mutton chop' hangers and the intermediate ashpan doors were also omitted, both of which may be seen in some close-up views, and a sand gun was fitted on the boiler backplate, which may be visible in cab views.

No. 5473 which was the second of the wartime engines built in May 1943 at Derby. These locomotives had the front smokebox liner plates omitted, hence did not have rivets around the lower part of the smokebox door ring, and the circular access holes and covers in their cylinder clothing were enlarged. Their connecting rods were shorter than before whereas the piston rods, slidebars and union links

were longer. Coupling rods were fluted and the injector bodies were fitted with drain cocks. With the exception of the smokebox front liners, all these modifications were applied to subsequent engines.

Nos. 4784 and 4793 built in April and August 1947 at Horwich. These engines were part of Horwich orders 98 and 99 built to Lot 187 from which the smokebox front liner plates were omitted again. Compared with No. 5473, fabricated valve spindle crosshead guides were used in place of cast ones, the boilers had top feeds on the first barrel ring, and there were extra washout plugs just behind the smokebox. Split pins on the brake hanger top pins were replaced by clips and round-

No. 4784 was built at Horwich Works in April 1947 with a boiler having the top feed on the first barrel ring and centrally-mounted non-return valve clacks without setscrews or raised cover. It did not have smokebox front liner plates — hence no rivets around the bottom of the door ring — and all its axles were solid. Its tender was a part-welded type and although it was built with external sieve boxes, they are obscured by steam in this view. Engine and tender were painted in LMS 1946-style livery and there was a small 'x' underneath the power classification on the cab side. The only meaning of this that we know of was to indicate engines converted to oil burning in 1947, which 4784 patently was not. At least one other locomotive, 4783, had the same feature and, like 4784, was stationed at Carlisle Upperby. We can add no more and would be grateful for any help readers could offer.          O. S. NOCK

In April 1955, No. 44784 received a boiler with top feed on the second ring at St. Rollox and was photographed there just after its repair was finished. It retained this type of boiler until at least May 1963. The engine was built with a rocking firegrate, the operating linkage for which can be seen alongside the firebox just above the platform, and when the picture was taken was coupled to a Mk 2 welded tender. As was usual at St. Rollox when 44784 was repainted there, the cabside numbers were applied in 10in transfers and the power classification was immediately above them.          A. G. ELLIS

*Another of the 1947 Horwich engines built with solid axles was 4793, seen here a few months after entering service at Polmadie. The forward top feed had no setscrews to the clacks, extra washout plugs were fitted to the front of the first barrel ring, and the smokebox door carried an 'SC' plate.* AUTHORS' COLLECTION

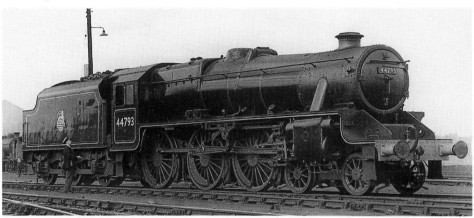

*From July 1952 to February 1957, No. 44793 was fitted with a boiler having the top feed on the second ring. As can be seen in this study, the top feed was the last type used on Class 5s that had standard clack cages retained by enlarged caps with standard clamping setscrews and raised covers over them. It had been painted and lined at St. Rollox with early BR emblems on the tender and 10in numerals on the cab sides.* R. K. BLENCOWE

head rivets were used on their buffer beams. Front cab windows were fixed without wooden frames and the beading was flat. Self-cleaning smokeboxes, hopper ashpans and rocking grates were fitted. The tenders were part-welded types with altered spring links and external sieve boxes. The locomotives were part of the Horwich batch built with solid coupled axles.

Nos. 44698 and 44701 built in July and August 1948 respectively at Horwich with forward top feed boilers. No. 44698 was the first engine to have what turned out to be the last alteration to the design of Walschaerts valve gear Class 5s when it was fitted with a new type of clackbox in the Ivatt-style top feed casting. Rather than the previous non-return valves, it had standard clack cages retained by enlarged caps with standard clamping setscrews that projected above the casting. To protect the setscrews, large 'top hat' covers were fitted over them. No. 44701 was identical to 44698 when built.

*Left: In February 1957, No. 44793 reverted to carrying a boiler with a forward top feed but this time it had standard clacks and 'top hat' cover. It was photographed in this condition at Kingmoor two months later. Note that the cylinder drain pipes were still supported at the fronts by a bracket from the cylinder cover.* R. K. BLENCOWE

The first locomotive built with what proved to be the last alteration to production Class 5s was 44698, which introduced the later type of top feed modified and fitted with a raised cover. It was also the first Horwich example of a plain bearing Class 5 having the longer, 27ft 6in wheelbase initially used for roller bearing engines in September 1947. Cylinder drain valves were the later type with altered operating linkage and pipework. A close examination will reveal the operating spindle for the hopper ashpan below the coupling rod between intermediate and trailing coupled wheels, which was a feature introduced with No. 4942 built in December 1945. The photograph, taken at Ferryhill in late 1948 or 1949, shows the livery used at Horwich on engines built there in July and August 1948. Stock numbers were displayed in white sans-serif characters similar to the 1946 style, reportedly 9in deep on the cab sides, and cast in the same typeface on the smokebox door plates. Power classification 4 was immediately below the cabside numbers and 'BRITISH RAILWAYS' was on the tender sides in white 8¾in letters with a long space between the words so that an emblem or crest could be inserted at a later date. Bottom edges of the letters were 2ft 6in above the platform. Locomotives built after this time had lined black livery with Gill Sans characters.

R. K. BLENCOWE

In September 1955 No. 44698 was preparing at Perth to haul the Bon Accord when this photograph was taken. It had received a boiler with top feed on the second ring in June 1953, which type it was destined to retain until November 1961, and the final pattern of top feed is shown without any cover. The engine had been equipped with a Manson tablet exchanger on the cab side and was coupled to a fully-riveted tender, having originally been paired with a part-welded one. Livery was typical St. Rollox style for the period. Rather than the expected light engine headcode, which it would normally have carried prior to being coupled to the train, the engine had two lamps in the express passenger positions.

AUTHORS' COLLECTION

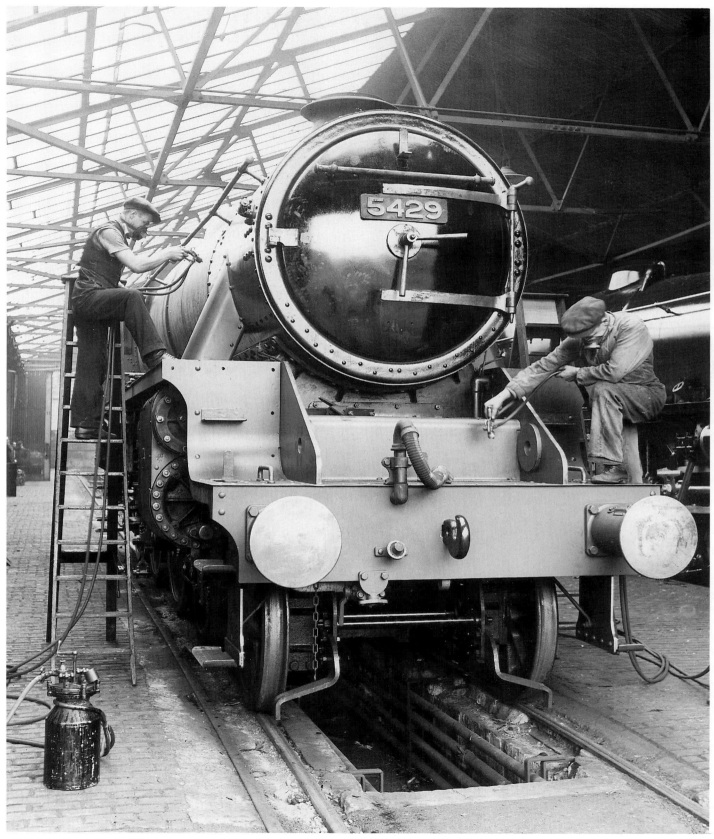

*This view shows No. 5429 being spray painted at Armstrong Whitworth's Scotswood Works. The photograph was possibly taken to show the use of spray guns, which was still unusual at the time when many locomotives were still hand-painted, but seems to have been posed as there is no paint visible issuing from the nozzles.*

NATIONAL RAILWAY MUSEUM (DY 22975)

# LIVERY DETAILS

*Any of the Armstrong Whitworth engines repainted before the outbreak of war received scroll-and-serif transfers with 12in numerals still in the low position and were lined out. During the early war years, however, lining was omitted and whilst Crewe carried on applying 12in numbers, St. Rollox used 10in ones, which were possibly imitation gold, shaded vermilion rather than lake and vermilion. This photograph of 5364 taken some time after the introduction of extra washout plugs at the front of the boiler barrel in January 1944 would seem to support that view. Smokebox door plates remained sans serif unless replacements were required but we have not yet seen one. As well as the change of boiler, the engine had been fitted with a bracket for a tablet exchanger on the cab side and had swapped its welded Mk 2 tender for a riveted Mk 1.*     R. K. BLENCOWE

The Armstrong Whitworth engines were the largest continuous series of LMS locomotives to carry the 1936-style sans-serif tender lettering and cabside numbers in gold, shaded vermilion transfers. Painting and lining details were as described for the 5000–5224 series in *Profile No. 5* and its supplement, cabside lining being limited to the front, lower and rear edges and omitted from the windows. Letters were 14in high with their lower edges 2ft 6in above the platform, the 'M' above the middle wheel and the other letters spaced from it at 60in between centres. Cabside numbers were 10in high with slightly varying positions. Most had their centrelines coincident with the centre of the main platform angle but on a few engines they were an inch or two higher. They were also painted in 2in black numerals inside the cab just above the windows on each side. The power classification was in 2in gold characters, '5P' immediately below the

side screens and '5F' underneath that. Smokebox door number plates were cast with sans-serif characters similar, but not identical, to the transfers; shed code plates were slightly different again and we think that the background to the rectangular Armstrong Whitworth makers' plates was red. As well as the standard bright metal items of the 1936 livery, Armstrong Whitworth engines also had polished smokebox door hinges, straps and locking handles, handrails and grab rails.

The 1938 Crewe locomotives in the 5452–5471 series were built after the reversion to scroll and serif characters and carried, we think, the old imitation gold 'countershaded' vermilion and lake type rather than chrome yellow, shaded vermilion examples. Letters were again 14in positioned as before but cabside numbers were 12in. Power classification and smokebox door numberplates were also scroll-and-serif. Shedplates were as before and

makers' plates had black backgrounds. Smokebox door hinges, straps and locking handles, handrails and grab rails were painted black. In later years, a few locomotives had the corners of their number plates and/or smokebox door hinges, straps and locking handles painted white or silver.

Any of the Armstrong Whitworth engines repainted before the outbreak of war received scroll-and-serif transfers in the same positions as 5452–5471. They also had the extra details previously noted as polished metal painted black. After the outbreak of war, the lining was omitted from repainted engines and colours, sizes and positions of characters varied.

Locomotives built from 1943 to March 1947 were painted plain black with scroll-and-serif characters but colours, sizes and positions again varied. Derby Works engines in the 5472–5499 and 4800–4825 series had sans-serif smokebox door number plates whilst those on all Crewe

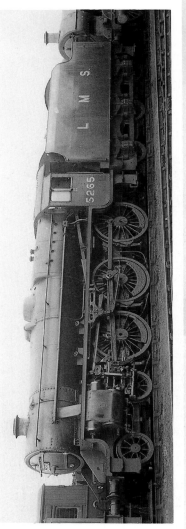

*No. 5265 was delivered from Scotswood in October 1936 and when photographed at Gloucester in July 1938 was still in 'as built' condition complete with crosshead-driven vacuum pump. It was still in original livery with 1936 block-style gold, shaded vermilion 10in numbers and 14in letters as well as sans serif smokebox door number plate and 5P 5F power classification immediately below the windows. Positioning of the transfers was standard and although both engine and tender would have had vermilion lining, dirt and the limitations of monochrome photography prevent it from being seen in this picture.*
AUTHORS' COLLECTION

*Locomotives built between 1943 and March 1947 were painted plain black with scroll-and-serif characters, some being yellow, shaded vermilion and others plain, pale yellow. Tender lettering was 14in high positioned as before and virtually all appear to have had 12in cabside numerals in either the high or low positions. Further details and examples are in the Profile. No. 4923 was built at Crewe in January 1946 and had yellow, shaded vermilion transfers with 12in numbers in the high position and power class 5 below them, as seen in this picture of it at Glasgow Buchanan Street about to leave with an Aberdeen express in June 1949 — it wasn't renumbered into the 40000 series until May 1950. From the angle shown, there are no alterations apparent since engine and tender were built.*
H. C. CASSERLEY

*LMS-built engines produced after March 1947 entered service in plain black with 12in cabside numbers and 14in tender letters in 1946-style straw with maroon edging and inset lining, smokebox door number plates having scroll-and-serif characters and power classification 5 being just below the cabside numbers. No. 4796 was built at Horwich in September 1947 and appears to have been in original condition when photographed with the addition of a Manson tablet exchanger on the cab side and fittings for a No. 5 snow plough. Although the tender appears to be a welded one, we believe it actually to have been part-welded. As can be seen here, it had external sieve boxes and, consulting engine and tender history cards, we can find no record of 4796 being coupled to anything other than its original part-welded tender before it was renumbered 44796 in 1950. We have also seen photographs of tenders we know definitely to have been riveted or part-welded in which the rivets are invisible and so have concluded that this is another example.*
R. K. BLENCOWE

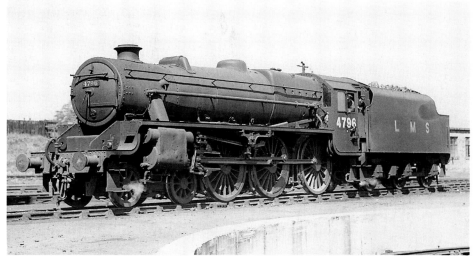

*On 30th January 1948 there was a parade of locomotives and coaches in various colour schemes at Addison Road Station, Kensington. Of the four Class 5s taking part, M4762 was painted in Southern Railway malachite green with black and yellow edge lining and 8¾ or 9in deep shaded yellow tender letters and cabside numbers, as seen in this photograph. Depth of the cabside 'M' was 6in and that of the power class '5' was 2in. The cylinder clothing bands were unlined.*
AUTHORS' COLLECTION

and Horwich locomotives were scroll-and-serif. Occasional embellishments, such as white or silver painted corners or rims of smokebox door number plates, could be seen.

In 1946, new-style sans-serif characters were introduced in pale straw with inset maroon lining and maroon edging. All locomotives built at Crewe and Horwich from March 1947 until Nationalisation, starting with 4768 and 4997 respectively, carried them when new on a plain black paint scheme, inside faces of frames, stretchers, axles, etc. probably being red oxide or bauxite. Cabside numerals were 12in high positioned in line with the 14in tender let-

tering and the power classification 5 was immediately below them. Smokebox door numberplates were scroll-and-serif on them all. A few repainted engines also received the 1946 livery.

In January 1948, four LMS Class 5s were painted in different colours at Crewe, renumbered with M prefixes and paraded at Addison Rd. Station, Kensington. Winner of the contest for mixed traffic and lesser passenger engines was M5292, which was in LNWR-inspired lined black. All post-Nationalisation production, with the exception of Horwich Nos. 44698–44701 that appeared in plain black during July and August 1948, were painted in this

scheme. The remainder of the Horwich 1948 batch, 44702–44717, had sans-serif, but not Gill Sans, smokebox door number-plates and 'BRITISH RAILWAYS' on the tender sides in 10in letters. The remaining locomotives had Gill Sans smokebox door numbers and varying tender-side embellishment, 44728–44737 being turned out with 8in deep 'BRITISH RAILWAYS', 44718–44727 and 44658–44667 having no lettering or emblems, and 44668–44697 displaying the larger version of the early BR 'monocycling lion' emblem.

The period immediately following nationalisation saw a profusion of livery styles for repainted engines, some of which

In this picture, the second of the Addison Road engines, No. 4763, is seen in the Crewe paint shop receiving its experimental livery of LNER green with black and white lining. Whilst the boiler and tender were being lined out, the front framing, platform and wheels of the engine were still in red oxide undercoat. The locomotive immediately behind 4763 also appears to have had an experimental livery but we can't determine its identity.
AUTHORS' COLLECTION

are illustrated in this volume. All were plain black but there were many variations of insignia including the short-lived M prefix. Some measure of order began to appear with the application of BR lined livery in late 1948 and early 1949 for all engines passing through the paint shops. Sizes and positions of numbers, however, still varied and there were several smokebox door number typefaces in evidence. Power classification became 5MT some time later and the occasional locomotive could still be seen with white or silver painted corners

to its smokebox door number plate. Despite the foregoing, there were still unlined engines running until at least October 1957. In the 1950s, Timken tender axlebox covers were painted yellow, those with grease lubrication having a horizontal red stripe for identification purposes.

From 1957, BR crests replaced the emblems, then, starting in 1960, overhead electrification warning flashes were added. After December 1962, repainted engines reverted to plain black except for those

emerging from St. Rollox, which continued to apply full lining to locomotives repainted there until it stopped doing steam work. Cowlairs also lined locomotives fully as well as painting their shed allocations on the front buffer beams and painting the rims of many smokebox door number plates white or silver. This is merely a brief résumé of the fairly complicated livery details and variations of Class 5s, further details being given in *LMS Locomotive Profile No. 6.*

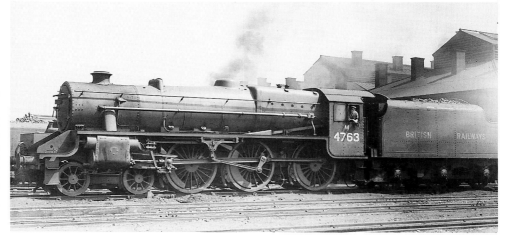

*In July 1949, M4763 was photographed at Crewe North in LNER green with black and white edge lining on the locomotive but inset panel lining on the tender. All characters were white and all except the 12in cabside numerals were the same sizes as M4762's. It was the only one of the paraded locomotives to have an 'M' added to the smokebox door number in the form of a small cast-iron extension plate.*
AUTHORS' COLLECTION

*M4764 was paraded at Addison Road in GWR green with black and orange panel lining on engine and tender but none on the cylinder clothing bands and originally had the same sizes and positions of white characters as M4763. In April 1949, however, it was renumbered 44764 and received 8in Gill Sans cabside numbers and a Gill Sans smokebox door numberplate, as seen here three months later at its home shed of Farnley Junction. At the time of the Addison Road parade, lining was only applied to the left-hand sides of the engines but on return to Crewe it was added to the right. All the green engines were built at Crewe in October and November 1947 and were unaltered when these pictures were taken.*
AUTHORS' COLLECTION

M4762 was renumbered 44762 in July 1949 and its Southern-style shaded yellow characters were replaced by standard cream Gill Sans ones, as seen in this view of the engine standing at Birmingham New Street the same month. Otherwise, its livery was unchanged and it was reported still running in malachite green as late as November 1952. All the green locomotives were fitted with Timken roller bearings throughout with, as this photograph shows, longer wheelbases and smokeboxes as well as slightly more protruding life guards in front of the bogie wheels consequent on the longer bogie frames needed to accommodate wider horngaps. They also had top feeds mounted on the first barrel rings with the redesigned casting and simplified clacks described elsewhere. Therefore, although there were no screws protruding from the shoulders, as in earlier top feeds, there was no raised 'top hat' cover either. The tenders were part-welded Mk 1s with external sieve boxes and Timken roller bearings, as shown by the circular axlebox covers. AUTHORS' COLLECTION

The colour scheme selected for mixed traffic and lesser passenger engines after the Addison Road parade was the Riddles-inspired black, lined grey, cream and red in a style more than a little reminiscent of the L&NWR that had been applied to No. M5292. The lining was altered slightly and the new version tried out on another engine, which we believe to have been No. 45225 when it was renumbered in May 1948. The locomotive was photographed twelve months later somewhere between Preston and Blackpool with 8in Gill Sans cabside numbers and 10in tender lettering. Characters on the smokebox door numberplate were sans serif rather than the true Gill Sans that was later specified for all BR locomotives. Apart from the livery, removal of the crosshead-driven vacuum pump, and enlargement of the circular access covers in the cylinder clothing, the locomotive was visually unaltered from its original form when built in July 1936 at Armstrong Whitworth's Scotswood Works. Note that the atomiser steam cock was still mounted above the handrail. AUTHORS' COLLECTION

No. 4841 was one of sixteen sloping-throatplate engines we know of that were given M prefixes between January and March 1948. Cabside layouts varied, the one shown here being applicable to just two black locomotives with 6in 'M's below the cab windows, 12in numbers in line with the platform plating, and 2in '5's below the numbers. Tender lettering was 8in and there was no prefix on the scroll-and-serif smokebox door numberplate. M4841 retained this livery until it was renumbered 44841 in April 1950. The engine was built at Crewe in October 1944 and it is noteworthy that when photographed its buffer beam was flush riveted; starting with No. 4826 built three months earlier, all Class 5s were supposed to have had round-head rivets.

K. J. COOPER COLLECTION
CTY. INDUSTRIAL RAILWAY SOCIETY

Another variation on the M prefix livery was the St. Rollox version with a 6in 'M' plus 10in numbers in one line immediately under the cab windows on each side. Tender lettering was 8in deep and all characters were white. Two engines are known to have received this livery and when M5476 was first repainted it did not have any power class figures on the cab sides — those seen here were a later addition. It does not appear to have had a prefix plate on the smokebox. Since being built at Derby in June 1943, it had received a boiler with extra washout plugs at the front and had a tablet exchanger fitted to its cab side.

R. K. BLENCOWE

No. 44839 was renumbered as such in April 1948 when tenders were being lettered 'BRITISH RAILWAYS'. At first glance it looks as though the painter was interrupted in his work when it came to 44839's tender but a closer examination shows that the rest of the wording was all but obscured beneath a layer of grime from which enough had been cleaned to reveal the first letters. Patches of the cab side had also been semi-cleaned to show the stock number. Before these token efforts, the engine must have lent new meaning to the term 'plain black livery'. Cabside numbers were in a style that was fairly common on locomotives renumbered without going through the paint shops during 1948 and early 1949 and which was based on the 1946 LMS pattern without edging or lining. Crewe used a straw colour on engines with 'BRITISH RAILWAYS' lettered tenders whereas it was reported that those applied at St. Rollox were white until about September 1948. Further details are in the Profile.

AUTHORS' COLLECTION

Nos. 44702-44717, built at Horwich in 1948, had the first iteration of BR lined black livery. As well as the red, cream and grey lining in panels on cab and tender sides and along the platform angle, boiler and cylinder clothing bands were edged with ¼in red lines. Stock numbers were on the cab sides in 8in cream Gill Sans characters with their lower edges just above the line of the platform and the power classification immediately below in the same style. Smokebox door numberplates, however, were not Gill Sans but another sans serif style. 'BRITISH RAILWAYS' appeared on the tender sides in 10in letters with a gap between words so that an emblem could be inserted at a later date. The lining at the front of the platform angle followed the downward curve just behind the buffer beam in keeping with Horwich practice whereas other works carried it straight across to the beam. No. 44703 was one of the few engines built with a top feed having an extended cover and was almost in original condition when this picture was taken at Balornock. The one alteration we can see is that it had been fitted with solid coupled axles.

R. K. BLENCOWE

*The livery selected for mixed traffic and lesser passenger engines after the Addison Road parade of January 1948 was lined black based on L&NWR practice before the 1923 Grouping and was inspired by Robin Riddles. The engine that wore the winning scheme was M5292, which is seen here after it had been back to Crewe and had lining applied to the right-hand side. Cabside numbers were unlined, 12in LMS 1946-pattern, their centre-lines being level with the platform, with a 6in 'M' above and 2in '5' below; 'BRITISH RAILWAYS' was painted on the tender sides in 8¾in sans serif letters, all characters being white. There was no prefix on the smokebox door numberplate, which was the original sans serif one fitted by Armstrong Whitworth. The cab side was edge lined rather than the panel style actually adopted for widespread application and continued up to the eaves.*
AUTHORS' COLLECTION

*Two months after the Addison Road parade, M5292 was the first ex-LMS Class 5 to be renumbered into the 40000 LMR series of BR stock. It had a scroll-and-serif smokebox door numberplate, 10in deep cabside numbers closely similar in style to the LMS 1946 pattern without edging or lining, power class 5 above the numbers, and retained its 8¾in tender lettering. The latter, however, was repainted as all characters were cream rather than white. The cabside edge lining was unaltered and lining was added around the slots and along the lower edges of the tender frames. It would appear that the tender frame lining was only cream and grey without the fine red line but examination of all the photographs we have seen of the engine in this condition, including a colour one, has failed to confirm it.* REAL PHOTOGRAPHS

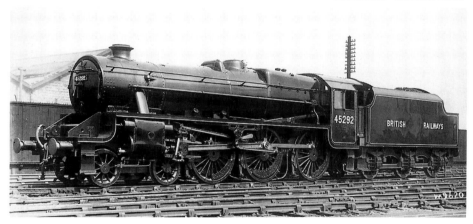

*For most of 1948, as well as into 1949 in the case of engines passing through St. Rollox, repainted engines were being turned out in plain black with a variety of number and lettering styles. One that we haven't seen before is shown here on No. 45411, which was one of the earliest engines to be renumbered and repainted following the introduction of 40000 series BR numbers in late March 1948. The cabside number appears to have been applied in 10in 1946-style numerals complete with edging and inset lining and tender lettering was either 8¾in or 9in deep. At the time it was photographed, 45411 still had its atomiser steam cock above the handrail and its left-hand crosshead was the type originally fitted when it had a vacuum pump.*
REAL PHOTOGRAPHS

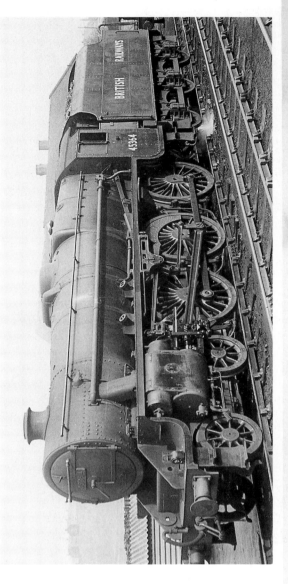

As already noted, styles and positions of numbers and letters varied widely in early BR days. A relatively unusual arrangement was the one seen here on 45364 with 8in Gill Sans cabside numbers level with the platform and 10in tender lettering on an unlined black engine. Instances such as this were usually confined to locomotives that were renumbered without passing through the paint shops but were simply patch painted. Since being built in May 1937 at the Scotswood Works of Armstrong Whitworth, the engine had gained washout plugs on its first boiler ring and had its vacuum pump removed. The left-hand crosshead had been renewed, the atomiser steam cock moved to below the handrail, and the circular cylinder clothing panels had been enlarged. Originally paired with a welded tender, by this time it had a riveted one.                    AUTHORS' COLLECTION

For a time after the decision had been taken to drop tender lettering, there were no transfers available for BR emblems and so tenders were painted and lined without any mark of ownership on their sides. This situation lasted from about the middle of 1949 to the end of the year or early 1950, during which No. 44666 was built at Crewe in the July. Lining was by this time fairly standard, except for the front of the platform angle, and characters were Gill Sans but there were still variations in size and positions of the transfers. Crewe favoured 8in cabside numerals positioned about halfway between the line of the platform and cab windows with the power classification below them, as seen in this study. The engine had all the external design alterations applied to Walschaerts valve gear Class 5s except roller bearings, electric lighting, double chimney and solid coupled axles, including a raised cover over the setscrews of its late-pattern top feed. Its part-welded tender had plain bearing axleboxes, short spring links and external sieve boxes.                    AUTHORS' COLLECTION

*No. 44680 was one of the last 28 Walschaerts valve gear Class 5s built, which all left Horwich Works between December 1949 and December 1950. They were turned out in lined black with Gill Sans smokebox numbers, 8in Gill Sans cabside numbers, with power class 5 above them, and BR emblems on their part-welded tenders. Note the Horwich style of lining on the front platform angle that curved down to the buffer beam rather than carrying straight across. All had long wheelbases with roller bearings to one or more coupled axles, 44680 being fitted with SKF ones throughout, and had long smokeboxes, raised covers on their forward top feeds, self-cleaning smokeboxes, hopper ashpans and rocking firegrates. The operating linkage for the grate can be seen alongside the firebox. Tenders behind all-roller bearing engines also had roller bearings, all of which were made by Timken, with circular axlebox covers.*
*AUTHORS' COLLECTION*

*From 1957 until about 1962, all repainted Class 5s had full lining and tenders were embellished with College of Arms BR crests, the right-hand one on 45480 being the heraldically correct left-facing version. The engine was photographed at St. Rollox in August 1960 having been fitted with AWS and a forward top feed boiler with 'top hat' cover that it carried from October 1958 to September 1962. It had been coupled to a part-welded tender with external sieve boxes.*
*P. H. GROOM*

*The Class 5s were excellent machines for working 'Maltese' partially-fitted freight trains, a duty typified by this photograph showing 5401 of Willesden passing Lichfield in July 1938. The locomotive was built at Armstrong Whitworth's Scotswood Works in August 1937 and, as normal during the summer months, was without its front steam-heating hose.*

E. R. MORTON

# LOCOMOTIVES IN SERVICE

*Class C express fitted freight trains in LMS days carried what may be described today as 'time sensitive material'. It could be something such as newspapers that would quickly become out of date, horses, or perishable items such as fish, meat, fruit or milk. In this view, 5378 is seen on Shap with such a train sometime in the late 1930s. The leading vehicle was a horsebox, followed by what appears to have been a gas holder truck. Next came a passenger brake van, six milk tanks, another passenger brake van, two more milk tanks and a further passenger brake van. The locomotive, which was built by Armstrong Whitworth at Scotswood in July 1937, was still in its original condition with a vacuum pump fitted, wearing 1936-style livery, and attached to a welded tender.*                                                   PHOTOMATIC

As remarked in the previous supplement, the LMS Stanier Class 5 mixed traffic 4–6–0s were remarkable and popular engines. Sir William Stanier was not noted as being a self-aggrandising man or given to exaggeration but when asked about the design in the 1950s, remarked that its popularity was due to it being, 'Such a deuce of a good engine'. The large numbers produced, operational flexibility and wide route availability meant that they were used on over 90% of LMS metals. In this context, it should be noted that the later, all roller-bearing, long-wheelbase engines had no more restrictions placed on them than any other Class 5s. This was despite weighing 4 tons 14 cwt more than the early vertical-throatplate locomotives and having a maximum axle loading of 19 tons 9 cwt as opposed to 17 tons 16 cwt. There were, however, some areas where even the early engines were initially too heavy

and programmes of bridge strengthening had to be carried out before they could be used. Two such sections were the S&DJR, over which Class 5s didn't operate until March 1938 because of weight restrictions on the Mangotsfield–Bath branch, and the Callander & Oban, which had to wait until eight months later before Class 5s took over the traffic from ex-Highland 'Clans'. The latter had earlier been displaced from their home territory by Class 5s and sent to the C&O prior to the bridges being strengthened.

Their flexibility, daily availability and mileage between repairs enabled withdrawal of many more older and less capable engines. Prior to World War 2 alone, 472 Class 5s directly replaced 596 ex-L&NWR, L&YR, CR and HR locomotives. They also displaced some classes of engines to lesser duties or to other routes, leading to a cascade that resulted in the

poorest or costliest to run being withdrawn. An example of this was the re-allocation and eventual withdrawal of the 'Clans' just mentioned.

In the previous supplement, reference was made to the permitted loadings for Class 5s over various routes and with differing types of train. To continue that theme, on the S&DJR section between Bath and Evercreech Junction, a Class 5 could take 270 tons unaided to Binegar compared with 190 tons for a Class 2P 4–4–0, 230 tons for a Class 4F 0–6–0, and 310 tons for a Class 7 2–8–0. At the other end of the line they could haul 380 tons into Bournemouth as against 260, 310 and 415 tons respectively for the other engines.

Following Nationalisation, Class 5s began to work further afield than the ex-LMS system. At the beginning of 1950, four were sent to Eastfield and tried on the ex-NBR and LNER West Highland line, where they met a hostile reception and were declared to be poor steamers before being relegated to third-class duties. Contemporary comment blamed prejudice among ex-LNER footplatemen and by March 1952 the engines were back, working regularly and successfully to Fort William. From 1951 to 1953, three were recorded as being stationed at St. Margaret's, Edinburgh. For a month during the early summer of 1953, seven Class 5s were on loan to the Southern Region when axle problems caused temporary withdrawal of the Bulleid Pacifics. During the 1960s, they also operated to the west of Gloucester and south of Bristol over ex-GWR lines.

Mixed traffic Class 5s were involved in several trials, both out on the road and at the Rugby Testing Station after it opened in October 1948. Initial tests of Nos. 5020, 5067 and 5079 during 1934 and 1935 were conducted to assess the engines' capabilities, the first establishing the need for boiler alterations to improve the coal consumption and later ones confirming that they had been successful. In 1937, Nos. 5264 and 5278 ran dynamometer car

*Less than a year after entering service, Nottingham-based No. 5282 was photographed with an express passenger train passing the foot crossing at Totley Pike. It bears all the hallmarks of an Armstrong Whitworth engine as built including flush-riveted buffer beam, small circular access covers in its cylinder clothing, cast valve spindle crosshead guide, and horizontal cylinder drain valves with all three drain pipes clipped together in a support bracket at the front. Its slidebars, union link and piston rod were the short variety whilst the connecting rods were long and coupling rods were plain section. The smokebox had front liner plates, there were no washout plugs at the top of the barrel on the front ring, and the early type of top feed was mounted on the second ring. The forward cabside windows were fitted into sliding wooden frames and the window beading was half round. It was coupled to a welded Mk 2 tender with long spring links. Like all sloping-throatplate locomotives, it was built with a hinged smokebox crossbar, door support bracket, short chimney, front steam heating and steam sanding. As with most of them, its coupled axles were hollow and it had a short wheelbase and smokebox. Along with all the other Armstrong Whitworth engines, it was painted in LMS lined black with 1936-pattern sans serif transfers and smokebox door numberplate.*

E. R. MORTON

*After trials with Class 5s on the S&DJR section early in 1938, six of the class were allocated to Bath in May that year. Regular working began with No. 5432 on the 10.20 a.m. Bath—Bournemouth train on 2nd May. This photograph shows the engine at Midford with a short Bath—Bournemouth train shortly after starting its service over the line. Lamp codes on the S&D were different from those on the LMS system, the one seen here indicating a passenger train whereas elsewhere at this time it would have meant a semi-fitted 'Maltese' — after June 1950, however, the BR codes changed somewhat.*

L&GRP

As we have remarked before, Class 5s were used on all types of train including express passenger ones such as that being hauled in this photograph by No. 4972 sometime in 1947 or 1948. Built at Crewe in May 1946, No. 4972 was equipped with a rocking firegrate, the operating rod for which can be seen above the platform alongside the firebox, and a self-cleaning smokebox indicated by the letters 'SC' painted just below the smokebox door locking handles. Stationed at Perth, the engine was fitted for the attachment of a No. 5 snowplough, as shown by the bolt holes in the buffer beam and brackets below it. Livery was one of the variations seen on locomotives built in the 1943-1946 period with scroll-and-serif cabside and smokebox numbers, the former being applied in 12in transfers in the higher position with the power classification 5 below. Although the numbers had recently been cleaned, we can't tell whether or not they were shaded.                                                        R. K. BLENCOWE

Locomotives repainted during the war were plain black and often only patch painted. Cabside numbers were typically scroll-and-serif with or without shading and generally appeared in the position seen here on No. 5283. The engine was stationed at Shrewsbury and was in charge of an ordinary passenger train when photographed.

AUTHORS' COLLECTION

Whilst not actually stationed on the S&DJR section, No. 4855 often worked over the line from its home shed of Bristol during the late 1940s. It is seen here at Bournemouth carrying the S&D passenger train headcode of one lamp at the base of the chimney and one over the left-hand buffer. The train consisted typically of Southern Railway coaching stock and Whitaker tablet exchanging apparatus was clamped to the left-hand tender commode handrail to facilitate transit over single-line sections. Although we don't have a date for the photograph, it would appear to have been taken during the summer months as the engine was without its front steam-heating hose. The locomotive seems to have been unaltered since it was built at Crewe in December 1944.        R. K. BLENCOWE

The first locomotive built with a sloping-throatplate boiler was Armstrong Whitworth No. 5225, which was renumbered 45225 and, we believe, repainted in lined black livery in May 1948. It is seen in this view hauling a Liverpool–Newcastle express at Luddendenfoot on the ex-L&YR line to the east of Hebden Bridge on an unspecified date. The second and subsequent coaches in the train were in carmine and cream, colloquially known as 'blood and custard', that had appeared at the Addison Road parade of potential stock liveries in January 1948 but was not then included in subsequent public opinion trials. From about the middle of 1949, however, it became the standard express train coach paint scheme. Whilst the engine appears at first glance to be 'ex-works', a closer examination suggests that although immaculately turned out with smokebox door locking handles, cylinder end covers and valve chest covers polished, it has, in fact, weathered a little. It would seem, therefore, that it had recently been cleaned much more assiduously than usual in preparation for some occasion such as royal train duty. From the flowers and foliage in the scene and the colour scheme of the coaches, we would hazard a guess that the picture was taken in the summer of 1949. Note the sans serif characters on the smokebox door numberplate that differed from Gill Sans style.

REAL PHOTOGRAPHS

*This August 1948 picture shows M4820 on a Class C empties milk train consisting of six-wheeled tankers and churn van near Harpenden. The load was seventeen vehicles, which were arranged in classical milk train formation with the brake van being marshalled in front of the last four tank wagons in order to steady its riding. The locomotive was one of the few to carry the M prefix and had 12in LMS 1946-pattern, unlined, white numbers on the cab sides with 6in 'M's above them and 2in '5's below. 'BRITISH RAILWAYS' was painted on the tender sides in what was reported as 8¾in white sans serif letters.*
                                                                                                            E. D. BRUTON

*The headcode seen here on Crewe North-based M5374 in 1948 or 1949 indicated what to a railwayman was a 'Maltese'. It was described prior to 1950 as an express freight or cattle train with the continuous brake on less than one-third of the vehicles but in use on at least four vehicles connected to the engine. They were indicated in the Working Time Table by a small Maltese Cross — hence the nickname. The engine was one of 23 Class 5s we know of to have worn the M prefix used for a couple of months at the beginning of 1948. It had 12in 1946-pattern numbers midway between the cab windows and main platform level with 2in power classification '5's above them and 6in 'M's below. Tender lettering was 8in deep, all characters being white, and there was no prefix on the smokebox door plate. Apart from the livery and enlarged circular access covers in the cylinder clothing, the engine was visibly unaltered from its original condition.*
                                    AUTHORS' COLLECTION

No. 44661 was built at Crewe in June 1949 and was turned out as seen here at Sheffield without any lettering or emblems on the sides of its tender. Positioning of the cabside numbers with power classification 5 below them was typical of locomotives built at this time. Although fitted with plain axle bearings throughout, the engine had a lengthened wheelbase and smokebox but, contrary to some belief, the cab was unaltered, as can clearly be seen in this photograph. Other characteristics of these locomotives included top feed with centrally positioned clacks and raised cover on the first barrel ring, later-pattern cylinder drain cocks, and rocking firegrate. The latter is indicated by the operating rod above the platform alongside the firebox. In common with all engines built after the Armstrong Whitworth batch, the commode handrails at the rear of the cab sides had pillar fixing at the lower ends and, as with all construction after July 1944, the front cabside windows were fixed and the beading was flat with sharp lower corners. The tenders paired with these engines were part-welded Mk 1s with plain-bearing axleboxes, short spring links and external sieve boxes. When pictured in August 1950, No. 44661 was at the head of an express passenger train in Sheffield Midland station.
H. K. BOULTER

One of the last Walschaerts gear engines built at Horwich in October 1950, No. 44690 had an extended wheelbase with Timken roller bearings on its driving axle but plain bearings elsewhere. It also featured an extended smokebox, later-pattern top feed on the first barrel ring with raised cover over the setscrews, later-type cylinder drain valves and pipes, and fabricated valve spindle crosshead guides. When photographed at Nottingham Victoria in the 1960s in charge of an ordinary passenger train, it would appear that the engine had received a replacement smokebox. There was no 'SC' plate or painted letters on the door and it had front liner plates, both features differing from the original. It had been fitted with a Smith-Stone speed indicator and overhead electrification warning flashes had been applied. The tender was the same type to which the locomotive had originally been attached — a Mk 1 part-welded example with plain bearing and external sieve boxes. The first vehicle behind the tender was an auto-coach with end windows.
AUTHORS' COLLECTION

trials between London and Manchester to provide data on which timetable accelerations and maximum loadings could be established. After Nationalisation, two Class 5s were involved in the well-known but fairly inconclusive 1948 Regional interchange trials and later that year comparitive testing began of Class 5s with Walschaerts, Stephenson and Caprotti valve gears as well as single and double chimneys. In the summer of 1949, No. 44764 ran constant speed trials between Willesden and Rugby to establish loading limits for use by the Operating Department.

A Class 5 visited the Rugby Testing Station at the beginning of 1950 to try different lead settings of the valves and then from June to September, another series of

trials was conducted there with a series of blastpipe and chimney alterations to establish performance figures in connection with development of the BR standard Class 5. In 1951, comparisons were made at Rugby of Class 5 performance with clean and dirty boilers. In January 1952, trials were conducted between Toton and Brent with Nos. 44667 and 45342 double-heading coal trains and in March 1954, a series of tests commenced between Carlisle and Hurlford to establish the difference in performance between a Class 5 in 'as new' condition immediately following a heavy general repair and others in various rundown states. More details of these tests, the engines involved, the results obtained and their effect on the class can be found in the *Profile*.

As is well-known, Class 5s lasted literally until the end of regular steam working on British Railways standard gauge, two of them taking the last steam-hauled train from Carlisle to Manchester via the Settle & Carlisle and another carrying on to journey's end at Liverpool. It is also probable that the last locomotive to be in steam at a BR depot was a Class 5. During their service, they had been used on everything from local trip workings to mineral trains, fast fitted freights, ordinary passenger and express passenger duties and even royal trains. In this volume we have tried to record some of the various trains on which they could be seen and some of the lines over which they ran.

*This view shows 1945 Horwich-built No. 44935 at the head of a Class C express freight train pipe fitted throughout with at least half the vehicles having vacuum brakes at Tring in April 1952. The Class 5s excelled at duties such as this and 44935 would have been regularly rostered to these trains from its home shed of Longsight. The engine was in 'as built' condition apart from its livery, which was lined BR black with the first type of emblem on the tender sides.*
R. H. G. SIMPSON

*When No. 44943 was photographed near Ais Gill in October 1953 it was running under a Class H headcode, which indicated that it was hauling a through freight or ballast train not classifiable under any of the other train descriptions. In this case, the rear four wagons were carrying armoured military vehicles. The engine was built at Horwich in December 1945 with a self-cleaning smokebox, as indicated by the 'SC' plate, and a rocking firegrate, although the operating lever for the latter is hidden by the mechanical lubricators. When built, the locomotive was coupled to a Mk 1 part-welded tender but by the time this photograph was taken it had a Mk 2 welded one.* AUTHORS' COLLECTION

*On Sunday, 26th April 1953, No. 44847 was photographed approaching Buxton from Derby with an ordinary passenger train. Built at Crewe in November 1944, the engine appears to have received an earlier-pattern smokebox with the atomiser steam cock mounted above the handrail.*

E. D. BRUTON

*Whilst Class 5s were quite powerful locomotives, there were some routes that required two of them to haul a heavy express passenger train, one such being the ex-Highland Railway route over the Pass of Killiecrankie and Druimuachdar Summit. A standard working was for two engines to take the down Perth–Inverness express as far as Aviemore where the train was divided into two portions. One engine would then haul the first portion to Inverness via Carr Bridge whilst the other went over the Forres route. Nos. 45357 and 44801 were photographed in the early 1950s at Blair Atholl with such a train. The former had received a later-pattern boiler with forward top feed having raised 'top hat' cover and was fitted for the attachment of a No. 5 snow plough as well as having tablet exchanging apparatus on the cab side. The atomiser steam cock on the side of the smokebox had been moved to the lower position below the handrail and was without a cover. The livery was typical of an engine painted at St. Rollox with 10in cabside numbers raised to clear the exchanger.* A. G. ELLIS

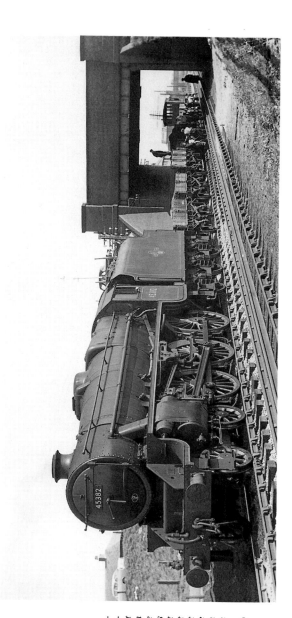

*Whilst it may appear that No. 45382 was displaying a Class J mineral or empty wagon train headcode when it was photographed in May 1958 at St. Anne's, it was actually propelling a ballast train and had a red tail lamp on its buffer beam. The shed code plate indicates that the engine was stationed at Carlisle Upperby. Since being built it had lost both its vacuum pump and the support bracket at the front of the cylinder drain pipes but had gained two washout plugs at the front of the boiler barrel and a later-pattern top feed with raised cover. The livery was fully-lined black with post-1956 BR crests on the Mk 2 welded tender.* D. T. GREENWOOD

*No. 45455 was one of the pre-war Crewe engines and was originally fitted with a boiler having the top feed on the second ring. By the time this photograph was taken showing it heading an ordinary passenger train in the late 1950s, however, it had acquired a later-pattern boiler with raised cover top feed on the first ring. The tender was the same welded Mk 2 type originally paired with the engine and had post-1956 crests on its sides.*
K. FIELD

*No. 44850 was stationed at Motherwell when it was photographed in August 1962 at the head of a Class H through freight train passing Lamington on the Caledonian main line between Carstairs and Beattock. Built at Crewe in November 1944, it was one of the Lot 140 engines beginning with 4826 from Crewe and 4807 from Derby that introduced round-head rivets on the buffer beam, fabricated valve spindle crosshead guides, fixed front cabside windows with no wooden frames, and flat window beading with sharp lower corners as well as other internal modifications. Crewe-built locomotives had front smokebox liner plates with rivets around the lower part of the door ring whereas those from Derby did not. Since being built, the engine had been fitted with AWS and had acquired a riveted tender in place of the welded one to which it was originally coupled.*
D. P. ROWLAND